How to Become a Better Long-[

MW00447661

Firstly, I would like to sincerely thank you for buying my book! It will give you the most important information to help you get started and allow you to start enjoying longer motorcycle trips. I have organized this into logical chapters to make it easy for you to navigate your way through this guide, and to help you find exactly what you might need quickly. I really hope that it will help you to become better long-distance rider so that you can begin to experience exactly how I feel now about long distance riding.

What to Expect

In this book, I open-up about everything that I have learned throughout my extensive years spent on the back of a bike. I share tips on preparations, equipment, staying safe, and more importantly, I do this in a no-nonsense way, sharing some of my stories from my travels along the way. By the time you reach the end, you will have many years' worth of knowledge, from my experience under your belt.

Remember: Focus on the trip, not on the bike, it is just a tool to help you complete your goals!

The texts features in this book belong to Pavlin Zhelev and they are protected by the Copyright Law and other such related rights. The registered ISBN number is: 9781370195466

Table of Contents

As I already said I have organized this into logical chapters to make it easy for you to navigate your way through this guide, and to help you find exactly what you might need quickly by simply clicking to the links below.

Top 10 things you need to take on a long motorcycle trip

How to choose the right riding gear for a long trip?

Camping Gear – What do you really need?

What tires do I need for my trip?

What to take and how to pack for long trip?

Top 10 tips for riding your motorcycle over a long distance

Top 10 accessories you should have on a long trip

Money for motorcycle trip – Cash or credit cards?

Navigation - GPS or Paper map?

Top 5 common mistakes on a long trips - How to avoid them?

Top 10 Tips to stay warm and dry

How to cross international borders with a motorcycle?

Top 3 ways to arrange accommodation for long trip

Crash bars and crash protectors. Are they really worth it?

When the Adventure goes wrong

Motorcycle riding and life insurance – Is it worth it?

The best way to prepare your body for a long trips

How to ride a motorcycle in hot areas?

How to stay healthy on a long motorcycle trip?

Top 5 things you should never do on a long motorcycle trip

Top 5 Myths about the long motorcycle trips

The world is so big but, the time that we have on earth is so little...

Who am I, and why should you trust me? I am just an average guy with a bike, who wanted to change his routine existence by setting out and pursuing a dream. Entering a new world, a world quite different, so unknown, and waiting to be explored.

About fifteen years ago I decided that I had to see the world and I had no intention of delaying it any longer. How? By riding a motorcycle of course, how else? The reason I chose to pursue my dream of traveling the world on a motorcycle is that, well, we all have our preferences. Some like to travel luxury - flying only first class, others think that buses are the most rational and practical choice. A few cycle like crazy and find it of great enjoyment! I owned a motorcycle, and I discovered that whenever I was riding it, I felt so relaxed and at ease. I literally used it as my antidepressant.

Some people said that I had lost my mind and gone crazy. Maybe it was a little crazy and impulsive at the time, but please tell me; can you honestly think of anything you have done in the past decade that fulfilled one of your lifelong dreams or even come close?

I was born in 1974 in Bulgaria (Eastern Europe). The first time that I jumped on a bike was in 1988 at the young age of just 14 years old. At that time, my country was part of the communistic bloc. You can imagine, (actually, you probably can't without taking a search through Google), what type of motorcycles we had. The first two-wheeled vehicle I have tried was Bulgarian brand called " Balkan." The next one was Russian brand called Karpati. Soon after that, I bought my first bike, from an East German brand called Simson.

So, this is how my passion for motorcycles began. Throughout the years, I have changed brands and overall, owned and ridden many bikes. I started off with these funny, small machines, then progressed onto faster sports bikes; I have even ridden a Chopper and an ATV for a while. But finally, I found my true calling and passion and decided to stick with touring bikes. Because I love to travel, this option was the one that suited me best. I have been so lucky to have discovered and ridden through some of the most beautiful and interesting places all over the world.

In last fifteen years, I have traveled on my bike through all of the below countries:

Europe
Bulgaria, Romania, Hungary, Slovakia, Czech Republic, Poland, Russia, Ukraine, Lithuania, Latvia, Sweden, Norway, Denmark, United Kingdom, Germany, Nederland, Belgium, France, Andora, Spain, Switzerland, Austria, Lichtenstein, Italy, Albania, Kosovo, Serbia, Macedonia, Greece and Cyprus.

Asia
Turkey, Georgia, Azerbaijan, Turkmenistan, Uzbekistan, Tajikistan, Kyrgyzstan, Kazakhstan, Mongolia, Russia + Siberia, Mongolia and China.

Africa
Morocco

North America
USA + Alaska and Mexico

The more adventures I am having, the more I realize that there is still so much to learn and even more to still to be explored.

I decided to write this book in order to help you guys and to make your trips much easier than my initial ones were. I did everything using a 'trial and error' approach, which is fine but it takes forever. As my father always said:

"To become a clever man first, you need to become an old man!"

Today, we have so many sources of information at our disposal so it would be a shame to waste that.

Anyway, I am not going to waste your time any longer, so let's get to it. In this book, I am going to give you lots of very useful advice about how to travel on long motorcycle trips.

Note: Everything I am going to tell you is based on my experience. I am not pretending to be an expert. However, I do have many trips and many hours, and days of experience. Everything I tell you all worked when I went on long trips with my bike, so I think it will work the same for each one of you.

Let's get started…

Buying a motorcycle – Expectations vs Reality

Every kid, young boy, girl, man or woman, middle age or even seniors, once in a while had an idea to buy a motorcycle or to at least try it. Even you, did you? Bikes have always been like a magnet for many people. A dream machine which will help you to feel liberated, and I totally agree with this statement. The feeling you get from it cannot be compared to anything else in the world. The expectations are so high, and they usually are not the same as the reality.

So, why is it like that? I will try to explain.

When I was just 15 years old, I already had some experience with motorcycles, and even then, I knew that one day, I wanted to have my own. The desired machine was a 50cc east German brand called Simson. The price of that bike was the equivalent of 500-600$ today. Of course, I was a kid, and I didn't have any money. I spoke with my father and after he heard all of my arguments he said:

"Ok, I understand these are nice bikes, so if you really want one, go and buy one."

That was great. But he didn't say anything about the money. Why? Because for him, it was not a problem to buy it. I waited a day a week, nothing. So, I had to find a way to earn that amount. Our summer school vacation was 3 months and I spend these 3 months, working on anything what was possible to work on, and to save that money. All of my school mates where enjoying their freedom and visiting the beach every day, I was working very hard. In the end I was able to save about 2 thirds of the money.

I was so disappointed, the summer was finished, and my dream was going nowhere. My father saw just how crushed I was and ask me what was going on? I explained, and he said:

" Now I know that you really want it, that it is not just a momentary desire, I will help you," and he gave me the rest of the money.

What I am saying here is, that almost everybody will like the idea of having a bike at some point throughout their life. However, only 30% will do what they need to do in order to buy a motorcycle.

Out of this 30%, only 10% will stick with the bike longer than a year or two, and only 5% will keep it and ride it for many years thereafter.

With that being said, let's discuss some expectations and the associated realities.

1. To get the drivers license is easy, you can learn the skills within just a day or two, and then you are ready.

Not really. Most of the younger generation do not have enough patience with this process, even just for a day or two. There are so many distractive things today, that to focus on something like that is not easy. Even if you know how to ride, you still have to be ready for the theoretical test. It is not that difficult, but you need to spend some time to learn it, and you need to be committed and willing to put in the hours.

2. Once you get your motorcycle, all the girls will love you.

Well, if you have a problem with this area of your life, then the bike is not going to help you at all. Maybe, some of them will want to jump on your bike for a while and maybe even go for a ride, but that's all. Is this what you are looking for?

3. When you have a motorcycle, you can take many adventures.

The definition of the word adventure is 'an unusual or exciting experience'. Did you hear something like that about a motorcycle? The adventure is absolutely a very special moment, and it is thrilling, but you can get equally as thrilling adventures with walking, hiking, pedaling, swimming, riding driving, diving, flying and many more...

4. When you ride a motorcycle, you will have so many friends.

It is the same as the earlier point I made about girls. If you do not have it until now, do not expect any significant changes.

5. You will look so cool and sexy in the motorcycle gear.

Really, who told you that? Do you have plans to go to the local coffee shop or restaurant with all of your gear on? Believe me, no one will understand you, or like you. Yes, they all will watch you, because it is not usual to see somebody, dressed up as RoboCop walking around. Try it, when your outside and it is 40C, and we will talk again.

6. With a motorcycle, you will travel faster.

In the City, yes. On the long distance, no. Your average speed will be 20 or 30% less than if you are driving a car. It doesn't matter how fast you ride. You might disagree with me now, but once you have taken some long trips on your bike, let's talk again. The weather, the roads, the distance, and the fatigue will slow you down day after day, and at the end, the result will be exactly what I have stated here.

7. Motorcycles are cheaper and require less maintenance.

It all depends on the brand and the model. With some bikes, you will be really surprised. Sure, some toll charges and taxes might be less for bikes, but on the whole, the cost elements can soon add up.

8. Motorcycles use less petrol, and It is cheaper to commute every day.

Again, this depends on the model. Do not forget the costs associated with having a bike are not only petrol. Some of the parts and accessories are far more expensive than average cars. When the winter comes, you will need a car anyway depending on your locate climate.

9. Your wife (girlfriend, boyfriend, father, or mother) will like the idea of your new hobby.

Really, ask first and I guarantee that I already know 90 % of the answers to that question, but you can try.

10. Motorcycles are fast, but you will ride slowly.

If this is true, then why are you buying a fast bike then? Is there no way to have a fast bike and ride it slow? Remember it – no way!

So guys, if you are new here and thinking that the motorcycle is only good fun, you are right, yes, it is. But you have to be ready to sacrifice something! You will decide what.

******

Motorcycle Riding Gear - Do I really need it?

Let's assume that you have just bought your motorcycle. You have sacrificed, and already spent out so much on it, and now you are wondering how important the gear is. Do I really need to spend so much money to buy all of that stuff? If you ever ask yourself this question keep reading and I will give you an answer.

Do I really need to have all of that gear to ride my motorcycle?

Guys you do not have to, you can ride your motorcycle with almost anything, even naked as I said in some of my videos. It is not a must, although there are laws to follow in certain countries regarding helmets and leathers. However, with the same result you can jump into the sea to swim with sharks with no protective cage; You can try to fight a bear with your hands, and it doesn't matter how good or bad person you are, what kind of skills you have or what exactly you are thinking at the moment. The end result will always be the same, you will be really badly hurt or even die.

This reminds me of one real story that happened many years ago in my hometown Varna, Bulgaria. Two local "heroes" got really drunk and decided to fight with a bear. They went to the local Zoo, jumped into the cage and started to fight with the bear. Of course, the first guy was killed immediately, and the second lost his eye and 50% of his face.

Motorcycle riding is a dangerous hobby and one that does come with the element of risk. You can ride without any gear for many years and have no problems. However, you are not Batman, Spiderman or whatever superhero you favor. You are human, just like the rest of us mere mortals, and, because of that, you have a brain, bones, skin, and internal organs that need to be protected. In the unfortunate event of an accident, even with full gear on, the chances of remaining completely unharmed are slim. Can you imagine what it is going to be like without gear? Is it even worth the risk?

Crashing without a helmet, even at very low speed in 90% of cases will result in death. You can't control your body or take a safe position because it happens so fast and the laws of gravity always work.

Sliding on the road at 100 km/h will almost certainly guarantee that you will lose at least 50cm of your skin and this guys, will hurt you much more than the price you are going to pay for your jacket or for your pants.

If you break your leg because you refused to buy motorcycle boots, you will have so much time to realize and understand how important they are while you recover. As I said earlier, it is much better to be in motorcycle boots than on crutches.

Losing the skin off your hands because you do not want to wear motorcycle gloves will put you in a very uncomfortable situation for the next 2 months and maybe until the end of your life. Let me give you one example:

Many years ago, I was riding on a motocross track, and friend of mine just underestimated one of the jumps and landed in a really bad way. He broke his leg, but what was more important, when we went to the hospital, and the doctor plastered him up, and everything was already done, he said that the leg was only hanging on by the flesh and the motorcycle boot, without it, his leg would have been separated completely.

The purpose of the riding gear is not only to protect you from crashes. It is also to protect you from various weather conditions. Let me give you another example. I was riding in Azerbaijan, and the temperature was more than 45 degrees Celsius. We had to zip our jackets, close all the vents and even close our visors to survive because it was so hot.

Can you imagine what it would be like to ride in only a t-shirt and shorts, you are going to burn like a chicken. When you ride in very hot conditions, your body consumes double or even triple the amount of water, and you are going to be struggling after no more than 2 hours.

What about if it is raining all day or if it is very cold. Motorcycle gear is designed to protect you in all those scenarios. Your new jeans or fancy shoes might be really nice to go to a restaurant, but not to ride your bike. You can find many examples on YouTube from people who were thinking the opposite way and because motorcycle gear is usually very expensive, let me give you some numbers:

A quality helmet will cost you anywhere between $200-$700. How much value would you put on your life?

A nice motorcycle jacket will cost you between $150-$1000 dollars. Let's look at this another way, only 1 sq. cm of your skin will cost you about $10.

I do not think it is necessary for me to tell you how much your lungs or hearts are worth, in my opinion, they are priceless.

Good, quality motorcycle pants will cost you anywhere between $200-$450. If you need to repair your knee, it will cost you more than $2000. I will say nothing about your ass skin! Yes, the ass has no soul, but you have and believe me you will remember it every time you have to sit down.

Quality riding boots will cost you anywhere between $150 to $400. Ankle repair will cost you more than $2000, and you run the risk of getting a permanent disability or even losing your leg.

All of those numbers are only the minimum cost you have to pay to fix just a specific problem, I am not talking about the total bill you have to pay for all of the medical treatment and for all of the pills and aftercare you are going to have in the hospital. Even from a business point of view, it is much better to invest before, instead of after an accident occurs.

So guys, the final conclusion is that you have to buy and wear your motorcycle gear all of the time. Even the cheapest Chinese gear will protect you more than the most beautiful air.

******

Dual sport or Street helmet - Which one is better?

Which one is best to take on a long motorcycle trip? So, let's say you have already planned your trip, the bike is ready, the money is packed, but you are still wondering which helmet to take. It is a very good question, and I will try to explain the answer here as simply as I can. Maybe the best option is to buy very well-known helmets like modular helmets from Schuberth. However, I know not everyone is ready to spend up to $800 for a helmet. I am not going to review the models from the entire marketplace because there are thousands of them; what I will do is just to give you a few ideas to think about.

Over the years I have used any kind of helmets: off-road, dual-sport, street, or modular helmets. You can find tons of information on YouTube and compare each one of the models if you so wish. They all have their individual pros and cons. Do not forget we are talking about the choice of helmet for a long motorcycle trip. What exactly does that mean? It means that the helmet needs to be comfortable, light, but safe. You will have many riding hours with this helmet, so you need to be sure that it is the helmet for you. It needs to be as quiet as possible, easy to operate, easy to lock and unlock, easy to clean and it should have the possibility to lock it on the bike, because some of the open face helmets cannot be locked on the bike. Your helmet also needs to be easy to forget in case it gets stolen, it will be difficult if your helmet costs $1000. After all that I have said, I will reduce the choice to 2 options:

Street and dual-sport helmets.

Let's start with the first street or touring helmet. There are many great options that can usually be found at very good prices, and with the prominence of the internet, it is now easier than ever to find thousands of models. If you spend a little bit more than $100-$150, you will be able to get a nice quality helmet which will probably even have a pin lock system. They are comfortable, quiet, easy to lock, clean, and store. Some of the models even come with integrated sunglasses which is a great added bonus. The positives of these type of helmets are very well known, so we won't talk about it in any detail. Instead, let me talk a little about the negative points of this type of helmet.

Too tight.

The biggest problem seems to be that these helmets are too tight. Because of this, it is very difficult for example to mount a Bluetooth system. This is not so much of an issue when you are riding a sports bike because you ride it for a few hours. However, this is all about long-distance riding, and when you are on a long motorcycle trip, you will have to spend hours or sometimes even days with this helmet on. Something that might at first seem insignificant, after only one long-distance trip becomes troublesome and just inconvenient. Please trust me when I say that I learned things like this the hard (expensive) way. I do not want you to have to go through these same mistakes.

Overheating.

When you are riding on a hot day, you will soon realize that these helmets are not very well ventilated at all. You have some air gaps, you can open your visor a little bit to breath, but the reality is that because these helmets are too tight, there is no room for any air inside. The air cannot circulate, and it is a major problem, especially in over 35-40 degree heat.

Not suitable for any terrain.

On long trips, you never know what kind of terrain you are going to get. For example, today you will be on a highway so the street helmet will be great, but tomorrow you may hit some off-road section where riding with a street helmet will be difficult. When you ride off-road with a street helmet and close your visor, it gets foggy everywhere. Even if have a pin lock system, because of the lack of air gap by your nose, your visor gets foggy, which ultimately means you will have to open it.

Another common problem is that if you need to wear glasses, it is very difficult to wear this kind of helmet. First of all, every time you have to take off your glasses and put your helmet, it is very difficult to mount it properly.

There are many more cons, but I hope that these are enough to convince you that for a long motorcycle trip, the better option is a dual-sport helmet. All the negatives that I just described do not exist on these type helmets. You have more ventilation and space and it not a problem to install a Bluetooth system. Most of the new models now come with sunglasses, so it should not be a problem to find the right one for you. With dual-sport type helmets, you can use goggles to ride off-road or in the case that you might break your visor. Of course, there are some cons as well to consider.

Dual-sport helmets are usually more expensive than the normal street helmets, they are not aerodynamic, and they are somewhat noisier.

Anyway, even with these negatives that I have just mentioned, I will always still prefer to have a dual-sport instead of a normal street helmet.

******

Visor vs. Goggles

Let's talk about the difference between a visor and goggles. There are many dual sports helmets where you can easily take of the screws of the visor and replace it with goggles to use it for off-road riding. I have seen many guys riding in the city with this type of helmet using goggles. I also tried a couple of times, and I found out that it is actually quite difficult to ride in the city with goggles. I will try to explain why:

Just to let you know, this is my personal opinion, I am not pretending to be an expert, and my opinion is just my opinion. Please do not believe everything you see on the internet. Try it, prove it to yourself and do not commit to anything before you are 100% convinced that it is right, and it works for you. This is just my advice from my own experience.

Okay, let's get back to riding in the city with goggles. As I said, I have seen many guys do it; I also tried it too. However, what I found out is that when I am riding with goggles, I do not have the same visibility. I lose a part of my visibility, especially on the sights. The goggles are made for riding off-road, motocross, enduro or maybe even supermoto. On those types of terrains, you do not have to worry about the traffic. You do not have to worry about the fast car coming from the left or the kid coming from the right; you do not need to worry about your side or peripheral view as much or as intently.

The most important issue with using goggles is that you do not have the same side view. When you are riding on a motocross track, for example, you are focused on the track in front of you, you know the track perfectly you know, every corner, every jump. You know everything, so you do not need to worry about anything. When you are riding enduro type in the forest for example, or whatever, it is the same story, you do not have to worry about the traffic, you do not have to worry about the things around you, you are focused on the track, you are looking about 20-30 meters in front of your bike and you're riding fast, that's all.

Also, when you are riding off-road or enduro, you need better airflow. This is ultimately why goggles are used, So that the air can come from everywhere. Another very important point is that with the goggles you never get foggy, if you close your visor just for a couple of minutes when you are riding in the forest, it will be foggy everywhere, and you will not be able to see anything. With goggles, this is never going to happen.

Another very important part is that the goggles are easy to clean you can just take them off and wash them quickly so that you will be ready for the next track. Also, the lenses of the goggles are very cheap if they ever need replacing. With the visor, it is a different story if you scratch it, you need to replace it. Depending on the brand, it can sometimes be quite difficult to find the right one for your model. The worst case scenario is that you might need to change the whole helmet because of the visor. If you break your visor while you are on a track, then you will have nothing. However, with goggles, it is much easier as you can carry spare lenses with you, so whatever happens, you will be fine.

As I mentioned earlier, riding in the city with goggles could be dangerous, you risk your life and the life of the people around you.

When you are riding with goggles, especially in colder weather, you are freezing the air comes from everywhere, around your nose, around your chin. It is also very noisy, and you have a limited side view. If I have to turn left or right, every time I do this, I have to turn more because of the limitation of the goggles. With the visor, it is a different story altogether. You can use your sunglasses if you choose, you can open your visor when you need more air or close it when you do not need it. With a visor, you also have a much wider angle of view.

******

Motorcycle Security

We love our motorcycles; it does not matter how much they cost. I know you love yours as much as I love mine because you are taking the time to read this book to help you master the art of motorbike riding quickly and efficiently. It is the stuff nightmares are made of. However, because of the desirability of the motorbike, getting your bike stolen is a reality we need to face. I do not want even to think about it. Read on to see exactly what you can do to prevent this from happening.

The first barrier against thieves is your ignition key system. It does not matter how difficult it is to unlock it, how many million combinations the key has or what kind of profile it is; it will be broken in just a few seconds. The thieves will use a special tool, known as a "breaker." It is a hard piece of steel, that will imitate the shape of your key. They insert it in the ignition, and with the help of a small wrench, they can rotate it to the right. First, they will unlock the forks, and then they will start your motorcycle. For them, it is so simple, and it will take no more than 10 seconds.

If you have a new bike, that was built after the year 2000, you might have immobilizer system. This system won't let the engine start unless the request for ignition is made with the original key. This feature is extremely reassuring, so now you can sleep well. Not really! If you have an expensive bike, like a BMW 1000 RR or a Ducati, you have to know that thieves have specialist software to start your engine without the need for a key. Second, because it is a bike and not a car; it would be very easy to push it out of your garage or even load it in a van. In order to combat this, you need to think of some kind of hardware to protect your motorcycle.

Let's check what we can find in the shops:

Ok, I will start with the simple cable lock. It is a very cheap option, but it can easily be cut in few seconds.

The second option is a disc lock. You unlock it, put it on your disc and lock it. The problem is that some of these locks can be opened with a simple pen. The rest could be easily destroyed with a chisel and hammer.

Then we have the serious boys, these are the more expensive device locks that come with a built in alarm system. If you move the bike or even touch the device, it will scream at 100DB and everybody in the neighborhood will hear it. Really! Let me explain something that you would not expect, nor is this information widely known. If you use a wet towel and cover the disc lock, it will silence it, and almost 90% eliminate any noise.

Another famous system is "Grip Lock". Basically, this gadget locks your throttle and front brake. You cannot move the bike, and you cannot move the throttle. Although this is smart, but the thief can easy

13

cut the brake line or the brake lever (it is aluminum, you can cut it easy) and the bike is no longer locked and secure. I think that any biker could ride without a front brake with ease.

For the rest, padlocks, U-locks, chains, or any other locking devices, I will show you a universal key, it is called a " Boltcutter.".. If the chain is big, perhaps something like 10 or 12mm, they will use a battery grinder. It will cut almost anything in under a than a minute.

If you lock your bike with a disc lock for example, and it is right in front of your window, any noise will wake you up. So, they cannot use a hammer, grinder or any other noisy hardware. But is this enough? No, because the thieves can lift the front wheel onto some slider or skateboard to move your motorcycle to a better location, where they can then cut the lock. In this situation, a chain lock around a post or tree would help.

So, now what? What exactly do we have to do to protect our motorcycles? We will get to that.

There is no such thing as 100% secure. This is the reason we have insurance after all. Even heavy-duty armored cars are only designed to hold heavy machine gunfire for about 5-10 seconds. Enough time for a professional driver to escape and save the passengers life. If he cannot do that quick enough, the result will be death for everybody who is in the car.

All locks, chains, and alarms are designed to slow down the thief. Once you accept this fact, the rest is easy. In your garage, you can install anything. Hook, chain, anything that will slow down or even stop them. When you are traveling, it is a different story. These big chains will weigh almost 10kg, and for that reason, it is not practical to think you can take it with you.

So, what is the solution?

Choose the one which will provide the maximum security. Lots of people have contacted me before writing this book to find out, what I personally use. I will tell you, it is no secret that I use a disc lock from ABUS. The name is ABUS Granit 68, and because of its round shape, it is near impossible to cut it with a standard bolt cutter. Yes, it could be cut with a grinder. However, I have already told you that there is nothing that is 100% secure. I bought it for about $150, and it was and still is worth every cent.

Just to let you know, I am not paid from ABUS or compensated for endorsing their products! I have tried and tested this product for my own personal use. I have had this a very long time, and I have always been super-happy with the security and robustness of the lock overall.

I am going to tell you now, eight very useful tips how to protect your motorcycle. They might seem completely obvious, but you will be surprised at just easy they are to forget!

Parking

Never, ever park your motorcycle in areas with no people. We live in the cities, and not in the forest. You can find so many better places to stop and park your bike. In front of the coffee shop, restaurants, shops. You can use the existing surveillance system in your favor. Any big office, bank, petrol station, or shop, has security cameras outside. Park your bike there, lock the disc and you are fine. Of course, it could be stolen again, with one of the methods I described earlier. However, it will be very difficult and almost impossible to do this without being detected. If you don't see it for yourself, the cameras will.

Parking spot

Never park a motorcycle next to the road. Go to the sidewalk, to a spot that is not accessible to cars Give enough distance between the bike and the street. This will prevent the bike from being easily loaded into a van or trailer. If they want to do it, they will need to push it to the street, which brings us nicely onto the next tip!

Disc lock position

Instead of locking the front wheel, lock the rear disc or the sprocket. Two people can lift the forks and push the bike. However, it will be very difficult if they need to lift the entire bike.

Use two locks instead of one

One in front and one on the rear tire. This will discourage the thieves, they are lazy and will quickly move on to look for another victim.

Cover the bike

There is a famous phrase, "the cat never drinks the covered milk." It is easy when they can see your protection and come back later with the correct tools. However, when they do not know what lies beneath the covers, this will deter them, and they might easily move onto another victim.

Attach something to the bike

Let me give you an example. If you sleep in a tent, you can connect some of the tent ropes to the bike. If they try to remove it, they will move the whole tent. You can also use some of the cheapest personal alarm devices to make some kind of trap and surprise the thieves into moving away from the back once these alarms are activated.

Put the disc backward

If you install your disc lock backward, facing towards the wheel, not to the street. This will make it very difficult to break. Yes, it will be difficult for you to access it as well, but I'm sure you will agree that the extra effort will be worth it.

Think like a thief

To protect your motorcycle, you have to think like a thief. I know that you are not naturally going to be able to do that but just try it. How you can take this bike now? What you can do in the current situation? Think! It will help you to find out where the weak spots are and to eliminate them.

The tips I just gave you cost nothing, but they could protect your bike better than any anti-theft device you can buy from the shops.

******

Motorcycle Chain Maintenance

There are so many and informative videos on YouTube that show you exactly how to clean and lubricate your chain. I am not going to teach you how to do it because it is a very simple procedure, and everybody can do it, even your children could manage to do it just fine. What I will do, is to show you a different point of view. I will try to push you to see the full picture instead of watching one very small point and spending so much time and money on it.

I will start with the most obvious of points.

The chain needs to be lubricated; with what, and how often is the question everybody asks. There are actually 3 different ways to do this.

1. Using engine oil or some other kind of grease. I never recommend this method because the oil and the grease collect a lot of dust and become almost like sandpaper; even more so if you ride off-road. Yes, it might be very cheap; but as a result, you are going to wear your chain and sprockets out much faster. In fact, it would actually last longer if you leave it without any care.

2. Using proper chain lubricant (spray). Spray it once every 300-500 kilometers and once per 3000-5000 kilometers, just clean it with a proper cleaner and then dry it and spray it again. I like this method. and this is more than enough, but we will talk in more detail about this later on. WD-40, I never use it to clean or lubricate my chain, for this reason only, I have no personal experience to speak of.

3. This is the oiler. Many of you love it because once you install it, you do not need to do anything at all. It just works, all the time without any problems. Ok, so it is not exactly like that, but we will talk about it in more detail later on.

Now, before we get started with the important part, let's have a closer look at modern motorcycle chains. There are many types of chains, but I am going to talk about the two most famous: with or without o-rings.

The o-ring chains have the same parts as the normal chains with one small difference; there are the small rubber seals. What they actually do, is to close the hole between the pin and the bushing and keep the factory grease in. The normal chains or the chains without o-rings do not have this, so the factory grease disappears much faster. Many of the dirt bikes use it, but I am 90% sure that your bike has a normal O-ring chain and it has a factory grease in.

The life of the chain depends on that grease. Once it is gone, the chain will start to get stuck, and it will not roll properly, meaning it needs to be changed. Do we really need to clean it and lubricate it all the time then? Yes. To clean it, and correctly free it from dust, preventing the dust from going between the rowers and the bushing and keep the seals in good condition. However, it doesn't really matter how often you are going to clean or spray it, it will not extend the life of your motorcycle chain.

As I said in the beginnig, the life of your chain depends on the factory grease on the inside. As long as it has it, the chain will be fine. Here many of guys will try to convince me that I am not right. You might say "the more you lubricate it, the longer it will live." That's ok, guys I am not here to argue with you, do whatever you like but over the years I have tried both: with proper care and without any care the result was about the same.

So how often do we have to clean and lubricate the chain?

This depends on you and your riding style. If you ride your motorcycle every day and it is mostly off-road in rain or muddy conditions, then you have to clean it as often as possible; but if you only ride it in the weekends, on sunny days once every month or once every two months, this is more than enough. I cannot tell you exactly how often you need to clean your chain because I do not know your riding style, but I can tell you what I do and give the same guidelines that I know work for most.

I use a dry lube and spray it once per week. I spray it always after I stop riding while the chain is still hot. I clean it and lubricate it properly once every two months; there are some exceptions when I am going to ride a lot of off-road or through sand; however, this is normally not very often. When I am on a long trip, I just spray it once per day. Later in the evening when I finish the ride, I spray the chain, and that's all. With this type of care and without anything else, my chain usually lasts about 20 000 kilometers, which is more than enough for me.

Now let's talk about the Oilers. For many of you guys, they are very important because the chain could last anywhere between 30,000-50,000 kilometers. I personally cannot believe that a chain could last that long. Yes, it would always look nice and clean, but it doesn't mean that it is factory new. The wearing process does not depend on the outside lubrication. It depends on the type of chain you use, the power of your engine, and from your riding style. If you race it, it will wear down quickly. If you are a gentle rider, it will last much longer. It doesn't matter whether you have an Oiler or not.

Let's get to the real numbers. Most of you will ride between 10,000-20,000 kilometers per year which means that once every 1-2 years, you have to buy a new chain. Good quality chains with sprockets will cost you at least $100, and during those 10,000-20,000 kilometers you are going to use five different sprays to lubricate the chain, all together this will cost you about $150. You spend a lot more for your Starbucks coffee, so if you cannot afford $150 a year for your motorcycle, just sell it and buy a bicycle, take the train or whatever. A good quality Oiler will cost you about $150. Maybe you will have to pay for someone to install it, and you will need extra oil and some more gadgets; so, all together it is going to be around $200. From this simple calculation, you see that the Oiler will cost you more and you are still going to have to buy the chain and sprockets.

Now you will resist and say "Yea, but after that, I can use it for many years."

Many years? How long are you going to ride this motorcycle for exactly? Ten years, are you sure about that? What is going to be your next choice? Can you use the same Oiler on your next bike? What about if you buy the GS1200 adventure with a drive shaft? Even from the economic point of view, it is much better to start the simple way, and just spray it. I am not even going to talk about the moments when the Oiler is not working properly and when all of your bike and the riders behind you look like a train from the 19th century!

My final words will be this:

Focus on the trip, and not so much on the bike. The bike is just a tool to help you on your adventures, and it is not the adventure itself.

*****

How to ride a motorcycle in the City

Come on, this is stupid, we know how to ride; don't we?

Interestingly, most accidents in the city actually happen with experienced riders, or at least with some experience. I will tell you why and at the end, I will give you 7 tips about how to ride in the city.

Ok, let's see now, experienced rider, what exactly does that mean?

 - If you have a license for 20 years, does this make you an experienced rider? Maybe, but some people, for example those in the military, are away for between six-eight months per year. Which means that they do not really have enough time to ride their motorcycles. When they return home, usually they will need to take extra care of so many things, and the last option is to ride the bike. Believe me, I have some close friends.

- Do you have a full-time job, from 10 to 6, with one free day – Sunday. Then it's the same story, you just do not have time for riding. One day a week is not really enough. And, it doesn't really matter what it is: Bicycle, Motorcycle, Car, truck or whatever. Do not lie to yourself, you just do not have time for it.

- Another tip: Fast riders. You can see them riding around the City at 200km per hour, making some nice curves and unbelievable overtakes with an inch of the cars. I will confess, that I also did that in the past. I was riding without any gear, no helmet, no jacket, no pants, just shorts and my tee-shirt was waving behind me as a flag. I was thinking that I controlled the situation and could do almost anything. A friend of mine said that I was going to be an organ donor. Now, I realize that I was just a very lucky/stupid guy, but many are not! You can visit the local bikers club or bar and you will be surprised just how many young people are gone, and for nothing!

- Dirt riders. Do they have enough experience? They can control the bike at any terrain, they can jump, and almost fly with their machines with no sense of gravity. Yes, that is correct, but do not forget that they do it with very light bikes, in a controlled environment. They have nice gear and usually do it for just a short time, often for only a couple of hours. On the street, they will need much more than just controlling the bike. There will be cars, people, traffic lights, rules and many more distracting things. So, they need to learn something completely new. Of course, the base they have will help a lot, but it is not everything and it does not make them experienced at riding in the city. The city is completely different on so many levels.

By the way, starting your career on a dirt bike is maybe the best you can do. Once you learn how to control the bike on the dirt, it will be so much easier to do on the street.

- Some guys will say that the experienced rider will have many accidents during their lifetime. Really, so they are saying that a rider with 20 crashes and 10kg metal parts in his body has more experience from a guy who has many miles under his belt without any accidents? I would say that the first should have stopped riding many years ago. It is obvious that motorcycles are not for him. It is just the same as a gangster who has spent 20 years in prison.

Stunt riders are the best. Yes, they are the best in stunt riding. It doesn't mean that it is the same on the street.

So, how do you learn to ride in the City? How do you make sure that you stay alive?

I will use one famous phrase:

"To become a clever man, first you have to become an old man!"

What I am basically trying to tell you here is that experience comes from practice. The more practice you have, the better experience you have. Which means that you can't just do it for a short period of time. The different situations that can occur while driving your bike on the road and off-road are so many that our entire life won't be enough to experience them all.

I am not saying that just because I wrote this book, I am the most experienced rider in the world. No, absolutely not! We all are learning. Every time, when you ride your motorcycle, you learn something new. Exactly in the same way you learn to read, write, calculate, to speak your own or a new language. It is all a matter of repeating. The more you repeat it – the faster you remember it, and at the end it will become second nature.

I will use another famous phrase:

"We are learning during our entire life, and when the fat lady sings we have already learned everything!"

Sometimes, I know that I am very boring Philosopher, sorry about that! It is now time to give you some more advice, which I hope, will help you to improve your riding style and keep you safe for many years to come.

N: 1 – Speed

The speed limit in the City is usually 50 km/h (30 miles), and in some, such as London, this has been reduced further down to just 35 km/h (20 miles). If you do not have a really good reason to ride faster, please do not do it.

If something happens on the road and you have to stop, you will need 9 meters for your reaction to kick in and 14 meters for braking. Altogether it is 23 meters.

If you ride at 80 km/h (50 miles), you will need 15 meters for your reaction and 38 meters to stop. Altogether it is 53 meters. You can imagine how much you will need when you are riding at either 100 or 200 km/h. The truth of the matter is that you are just not going to be able to stop, the consequences of this are likely to be fatal.

N: 2 – Distance

From the numbers, I just told you, you have to be clear that more distance is better. You increase the chances of both reacting and stopping on time. Anyway, even if you ride with two meters distance, it doesn't mean that you will move faster, but it definitely means that if the car in front of you stops, you will crash into it.

I do not think that I have to remind you of the physic laws:

"When two objects collide, the smaller object will absorb the energy of the bigger."

N: 3 – Position

Many people will advise you to stay on the side, left or right, and not in the center. This is because you will be more visible in the mirrors. Left or right could be very confusing for riders from the UK for example. I would say, always ride in the most visible position. Remember, for most of the drivers on the road; you are invisible! When you are changing your position or turning, never go before you are 100% sure that the drivers around you have seen you – even if you have the right of way. Right of way means nothing when somebody else takes it. This rule will help you with your insurance policy, but not with your life.

N: 4 – Control levers

It is not a problem to control your motorcycle with just a few fingers. Use the rest to help you in case of an emergency. Keep one finger on the front brake, ready to react. You can twist the throttle without any problem. Two fingers on the clutch, ready to press, if necessary. Adjust all the levers to the right position. To be ready to press it or just to hold it most of the time. This is very important! Adjust your brake pedal to the right position. If it is too high, every time you have to lift your leg, you are losing time or you can press it accidentally. If it is too low, you might miss it. In both cases, it could cost you a lot.

N: 5 - Filtering or Lane Splitting

One of the reasons why we choose the motorcycle for a city ride is the possibility of avoiding the traffic. I am not going to tell you to stop doing it, but you have to know few things:

 - When you are moving between the cars, do it slowly. When the drivers and the passengers are sitting in the traffic, they expect everybody to stay still. They can open the door without any warning because they will never expect somebody like you to come at the same moment. If possible, do it from the driver's side, at least they have a mirror. If necessary, use the horn to warn them. Do not think that your exhaust is loud enough. Maybe it is, but for a teen girl with headphones or someone listening to loud music, it is not.

- Do not press people if they won't let you to go. Some drivers are very nice and they will even make more space for you to pass them easily, but some are just morons or some people, such as old ladies do not know what they have to do. So please do not press them. You can overtake later, when you have the chance to do so safely.

- When you are riding between the cars, hold your legs on the pegs. There are few reasons to do this.

1st – You can use the rear brake if necessary.

2nd – You get better control of the bike when you hold it with your knees.

3rd – Is the one most riders will miss. When you are using your legs, you are actually moving your handlebar from left to ride, and you can't really hold a straight line. This will increase the chances to scratch somebody's car or cause a more serious accident. If you do not trust me, you can try it on empty parking. If, for any reason, you can't ride between the cars with your legs on the pegs, then wait in the traffic or learn how to do it.

N: 6 – Overtake

Choose a proper speed to do it. Not too fast, not too slow. Too fast - the driver in the car might not be ready for you. Too slow – he might forget that you are there. In both cases, you have to stay in the blind spot for as little time as possible.

N: 7 – Always wear your gear

This should be my first tip, but anyway I hope you will remember it better. Maybe I have saved the best for last! Always, always wear your gear. It doesn't matter how long you will ride for or where you go. Accidents never happen when we expect. Even the cheapest Chinese jacket will protect you better than a t-shirt from Gucci or Versace. A simple helmet protects you more than a New York Yankee's hat. You can buy new riding pants, but you can't buy new skin for your ass. You will look much better in motorcycle boots than in plaster and crutches. Any gloves protect better than the most beautiful air.

And my final words are: " **Never ride faster than your guardian angel can fly.**"

******

How to extend the Engine Life

If you have the chance to change your motorcycle every 2 or 3 years, the information I am going to share is not for you, but if you love your bike and you want to ride it for as long as possible, stay with me and I will give you some very useful tips about how to extend your engines life.

So you have a new bike. You made the proper break in. You checked the manual carefully and you did exactly what it said. You did it because you want to ride your motorcycle without any mechanical problems for as long as possible. That's correct, but is it the right way to do it? Is everything in the manual written for your bike, for you, for your country and your riding style? The answer is not that simple and to make it clear, I have to give you an example. The bike will be the same as mine - Yamaha XT 660. For this model, the maintenance you have to do is once every 10,000 kilometres. So, so once per ten thousand kilometres you have to change the oil (the oil is supposed to be 10W40 semi-synthetic, nothing special), and you have to change the air filter on every other change. So, if we look at it from this point of view, it's absolutely a simple maintenance and anybody could do it. That's okay, but what if we have 2 different owners?

The first guy, we'll call him John, lives in Alaska. Sorry guys, I know Yamaha refused to import this bike in the states so I am really sorry about this. So let's say the guy lives in Norway, in the northern part. The summer temperatures never go over 25 degrees, he rides mostly on the road. He never rides extreme. He keeps his bike in the garage during the winter and he does about 10,000 kilometres per year.

The second driver lives in South Africa, his name will be Mike. He's a racer. He rides his Tenere in the most extreme conditions you can ever imagine. He rides only off-road. He crosses rivers. He rides in the sand and the climbing hills, does serious off-road and is usually going over 160 km/h on the highway. He doesn't have a garage, so the bike stays outside even when it's raining or when it's cold. Mike also drives about 10,000 kilometres per year. According to the manual, they need to do exactly the same maintenance. The question is, which bike will last longer? You do not need to be mechanical expert to realize that the first bike will work much longer because the maintenance Mike does is not enough for his type of riding. Motorcycle companies sell bikes around the world, so they don't know who's going to buy the bike and how the bike is going to be used. So they have a basic line or the standard maintenance which covers most of the temperature ranges and riding conditions. But it doesn't mean that this maintenance is good or is enough for any kind of rider or riding style. So, how often you have to change your oil, depends on your riding style.

Maybe you will resist for a while and you will say: "Well, if it's written 10,000, you should be okay, I don't care about it. As I said in the beginning, yes, if you have a chance to change your motorcycle every three or five years, no problem, ride it and do exactly what is said in your manual. But, if you want to keep your bike, always in good condition and full working condition, then continue reading.

Most of the manufacturers extend their oil change intervals. So in the cars, it's supposed to be 10,000 km and now they have moved it to 15,000 kilometres, even 20,000 kilometres. In the UK for example, if you buy a new car, you have to change your oil every 25,000 miles. Can you believe this? I'm sure guys that each one of you who is from the states will now say: "25,000 miles without changing the oil?" Yes, correct this is what is said in the European manuals - 25,000 miles and it should be okay. I know in America, you change your oil every 3,000 or 5,000 miles, so what's the point? I'm going to tell you.

It started with cars, but it also started being seen even on the motorcycle maintenance channels. It was 10,000 kilometres, but I have seen now, that on a BMW it's 12,000 km, with some other brands it is 15,000 kilometres and I have even seen it at 20,000 kilometres oil change intervals. They will say that the quality of the oil today is much better than old, and that the engines are much better and so on and so on, but this is all bullshit. The engine, if we take for example one old BMW, like the R80; it is almost the same as today, the only difference is with the cylinder heads. The engine was 50 horsepower; today it is 130 horse power, so this engine works in much more stressful conditions. It works harder and the oil intervals are three times longer. Is there any logic to this?

To explain to you why it's like that, I have to give you one more example.

So, Germans are very practical people. They love calculators, so they calculate everything. Let's take for example Mr Hans. Mr Hans goes to BMW to buy a new BMW GS1200 adventure. Hans sits in front of the dealer and the dealer is explaining everything to him about the bike. When the deal is finished, Hans of course will have some questions: "How often do I have to change the oil and how much is it going to cost me". Of course the dealer will say: "It's nothing to worry about. First 1000 kilometres after that every 12,000 or 15,000 kilometre intervals. An oil change costs about 150 Euros. So, Hans will take the calculator and we'll calculate: "Okay I have a plan to ride this motorcycle maybe 100,000 kilometres. During this period, I have to change the oil every 15,000 kilometres, I will have approximately six changes. Six changes, 150 euro each - 900 Euros. That's okay. I can buy this motorcycle".

But if the dealer said: "Well, on this new BMW, you have to change the oil every 5,000 kilometres" Hans will be shocked and will say: Huh, every 5,000 kilometres so that means that for 100,000 kilometres I have to change the oil 20 times. 20 times at 150 Euro for each one will cost me 3000 Euros"; and he'll say: "No, the maintenance on this bike is too expensive, I'm going to the next dealer and will buy their bikes because the maintenance there is on 15,000 kilometres"

It's all about the marketing and the business? It's not about your bike. The dealer doesn't care about the life of your motorcycle. The warranty is usually one year or 12,000 kilometres. During that period of one year or 12,000 kilometres, it doesn't matter what kind of oil you are going use and it doesn't matter how often you are going to change it. The bike will work fine, but after that the problems will start, and they'll be probably with the next owner.

So what do we have to do?

The simple answer is this: Your engine life depends on the maintenance you're going to do. I will now give you some very useful tips which will help you to extend your engine life.

Number 1

Oil. The oil is the most important liquid in your engine. Without this, it will stop in just a couple of seconds. Change it as often as it needs. If you ride mostly on the road, then every 10,000 km periods is fine. If you ride off-road - sands, dunes, dust or in any kind of hard conditions, you have to change the oil no later every than 5,000 kilometres. If you race, you have to change the oil every 1000 kilometres or after each race.

Number 2

Use proper oil, which suits your temperature range. If you have plans to ride in hot areas like Asia for example, choose a proper grade oil. 10W40 semi-synthetic is good enough for normal roads, for normal temperature conditions like 20 or 30 degrees, its fine. But, when we go over 40 degrees, this oil becomes like a water and the lubrication, is not good. You will wear out the engine much faster and if you have a wet clutch, as most of the bikes do, you increase the chances to burn it faster. Full synthetic oils are much better. In the temperature ranges. The difference between 10W40, 10W50 or 10W60 is only in the warm. This means that if you ride your motorcycle in extreme cold conditions, with 10W60, you will have much better lubrication than with the usual 10W40. Believe me, I tested that many times. Of course, it is not so right to use 10W60 during the winter periods and with temperatures below 10 degrees. If you do, the bike will not break, but for the first couple of minutes the clutch will not be working properly. Once it gets warm you will be fine.

Number 3

Change the air filter as often as it needs it. If possible, buy a better filter like a K&N or other brand. These types of filters are made from foam and you can wash them after you ride, especially if you ride in sand. After that, you can go home, just wash the filter, lubricate it with special oil and it'll protect your engine from sand and dirt.

Number 4

When you start your engine, always leave it to work for a couple of minutes. Do not twist the throttle, do not accelerate, and do not start to ride it immediately. Just leave it to work for a couple of minutes. The modern motorcycle engines are made from thousands of moving metal elements inside. The oil is the only barrier between all these moving parts. Warm it properly. When the oil is not warm enough, it cannot lubricate well, so just leave the motorcycle to work for a couple of minutes for the oil to get warm and to have proper lubrication.

Number 5

Be careful with the throttle. Don't go to higher revs without any good reason. If your bike is calculated to the maximum revs of 8,000, 4,000 or 5,000, this is the level you should keep to for most of the time. It doesn't mean that you cannot accelerate to the seven or 8,000 if you need to overtake or to make some fast action, no, but I mean it as an example. If you're cruising on the highway, then 4,000 or 5,000 is more than enough if you plan to do this for a few hours. Because the engines are different, and their revs are different, some bikes have about 12,000, 13,000, 15,000 up to 18,000 revs. What you basically need to do, is to keep the arrow somewhere in the middle between the minimum and the maximum of your revs. When you're riding on high revs without any reason, you're actually wasting your money.

Number 6

Use the clutch every time when you change your gears. It doesn't matter if you shifting up or down. Do not listen to the guys from your neighbourhood with the fist bikes who will say that when you shift up you don't need to use the clutch, and don't look at the guys from Moto GP. They fight with the time and after the race, their engine or gear box will be changed. But you have your motorcycle, your engine, and your gearbox; if you want to keep it in good condition, use the clutch every time. Learn how to use the throttle to level the revs when you gear down. What you need to do, is to press the clutch, twist the throttle, and then gear down. It will give you more stability and possibility to accelerate faster if you need to. It looks like a very difficult task, but it's not. When you learn how to do it becomes like second nature.

Number 7

The engine break is fine, it's a good option, and it should be used. But carefully and with purpose. Remember the brakes are cheap the engine is not.

Number 8

Never twist the throttle before you cut the engine. I have seen so many guys that twist the throttle a few times and then cut the engine. This is the worst possible thing you can do. Your motorcycle engine, as I said, is made from thousands of moving parts, so just imagine all of these moving parts moving at about 7,000 revs per minute, being stopped immediately. When you do it, what actually happens is that you create small cracks in the metal parts and over the years, these small cracks just destroy your engine.

******

How to Winterize Your Motorcycle?

It is a very simple procedure that will take between 30-40 minutes, and everybody can do it. Keep in mind this is time well spent, all the work will pay off next spring when you try to start your bike.

Step 1.

First, you have to wash your bike to remove all the bugs, dust, sand, salt, and everything that is left from the riding season. After you finish, start your bike and let it run for a couple of minutes to dry. The best way to remove water from the bike is by driving it. Just 10 -15 minutes of riding will remove any water from the bike. Make sure it is warm enough, so all the water from the exhaust is already out. By the way, during this time you can go to the petrol station to fill the tank. You need to add a stabilizer to your petrol. The brand of the stabilizer doesn't matter, you just need to make sure you have enough for the size of your tank. Put it in and fill your tank to the top. Make sure you give enough time for the engine to get warm and to let this stabilizer go into your injection system.

Step 2.

You have to lubricate the chain properly. Make sure that you lubricate it right after you have stopped, while the chain is still warm. I use WD-40 to spread everywhere, on all bolts and all nuts, especially if your bike is going to stay outside. After you finish, you can clean the rest with a towel or some paper. After all of this is done, there is just one thing left to do. Some people prefer to change their oil before the Winter. It is actually the better way because if you have fresh oil you are not going to have this condensation during the Winter and you will prevent your metal parts from rusting. I used to do it before but not anymore. My engine is on over 100,000km, but it worth to do it on a new bike.

Step 3.

Lift the bike onto the center stand. If you do not have one, then just use a piece of wood or a jack. Just make sure that the tires are above the ground, and after that you can then disconnect the battery. When you unscrew the bolts, just unplug it and then put the bolts back in the same position right on the battery. When you do it this way, you do not have to worry about where you left the bolts in the Winter, so next Spring when you start the bike they will be in the same position. If the bike is going to stay out, make sure you have a nice waterproof cover.

Step 4.

Put the battery on the battery tender, make sure it shows 12 volts. Red for positive, black for negative. You can leave it for the whole Winter. That is all.

******

Top 3 reasons to go on a Motorcycle Trip

So, now you have the bike, the riding skills, the gear, you are now considering actually going on a long trip. You are still not sure about the decision you are going to take, and you are looking for some kind of encouragement.

Number 1:

You have to see the world. Everybody will agree with me that the world is great and we have to see it. Some of you might ask "Okay the world is beautiful, we agree we have to see it, but why with a motorcycle? We can do it by plane, by car, even the bus is more comfortable than a motorcycle".

Yes guys, you are right that you can find many more comfortable ways to do it, you can even sit in front of your TV screen and watch other people's videos, that's correct. But is this what you are looking for? You have to stand up, take your bike and just ride it. Break the routine of your life, take some action, step out of your comfort zone, and make something new, the motorcycle will give you everything you need. It's like a universal vehicle, a multifunctional tool or however you want to phrase it. With a motorcycle, you will be able to kill many birds with one stone. It will be your vehicle, your friend, your purpose, your goal, your pleasure, your future, your past, and the best anti-depressant you will ever have. The feeling you can get from riding a motorcycle cannot be compared to anything else in the world. You will feel every hole, every noise, every smell, and every gust of wind, including the bad weather or rain, but who cares about all these things when you have all of that freedom?

Number 2:

A chance to meet new people. I have said this before, but I am going to say it again. The best part of every trip is this great possibility to meet new friends. People from all around the world are great. Nationality, skin color, religion, beliefs, all those things do not matter, we are human beings and all desire the same things: health, food, shelter, and laughter for ourselves and our families. In the past, when people saw a man on a horse or a traveler, they immediately knew what he or she needs. Today we ride motorcycles not horses, but 99% of the people around the world will be happy to help you because they know what you need.

When using a different type of transportation, for example a plane or a car, it is a different story because you might come here for business or you are a tourist that is here to see the town or something like that. On the other hand, when you come with a motorcycle, it is obvious that you are going to be tired because you have ridden for so many days, and you just need to rest and relax. The best part of everything is that the people are usually interested in motorcycles even if they have never ridden one, they are still interested. They are curious about what it is like to travel on a motorcycle, how fast you ride, how dangerous it is, and many other things like that. This of course sometimes opens unexpected possibilities, and you are invited to be a guest in someone's house. And, when that person is from a different religion or whatever, you actually go into a new world. You will have the possibility to see life through their eyes. For just one day or one night spent like this, you will learn much more than from 1000 days spent in front of the TV. These are your adventures and your experiences, they belong to you and nobody else.

Number 3

The possibility to test yourself. Many of you are looking for adventure. You are happy to pay thousands of dollars for expensive motorcycles or special gear believing that this will help you to reach it much faster, but actually, you miss the whole picture.

The definition of adventure is an **unusual and exciting experience** which usually involves some risk.

Did you hear something about expensive gear?

Most of the expensive brands around the world use this magic word "adventure" to sell their product. Of course, being human we are easily brainwashed, and we start to believe this is the only way to reach it. The truth is, that once you step out of your comfort zone, you are actually testing yourself and you are going to have your own adventure. The motorcycle will give you this great opportunity. Yes, it is not easy, and you have to be ready to ride many kilometers in both good and bad weather. You will probably sleep in some shitty places, wearing the same clothes day after day, and miss some of your important rituals like an early morning coffee or the late evening news. But, I promise you, that you will come back home with a big smile on your face.

Of course, there are also some negatives: constant ass pain and an almost guaranteed addiction. Yes, you will be addicted, because when you do it once you will want to do it again and again because the long-distance motorcycle trips are the best thing you can do.

******

Long Motorcycle trips - how much do they cost?

How much does it cost to go on a long motorcycle trip? That is a nice question; the answer depends on many variables, but I will try to answer it as easily as possible. Keep reading, and I will give you some useful tips how to travel cheaply.

When people meet us on the road, they always think that we're some kind of millionaires seeking out adventure. They are right, but only for the second part. Yes, we are really looking for adventure, but we work really hard to be able to afford to travel with our motorcycles. When I plan a new trip, I always do a lot of research and find all the possible information for the destination I am going to. This gives me a chance to roughly calculate how much it is going to cost. So let's go to the main topic. How much does it cost? Let's split this into 4 different categories.

- Petrol
- Accommodation
- Food
- Other cost and unexpected costs

There is actually another one:

- Visas and documents, but we are not going to discuss this today.

We will calculate only what we need on the road. Let's start with the first:

1. Petrol:

Most of the bikes use about 5 liters of petrol per 100 km. 1,000 km is 50 liters. The average price in Europe is about 1.30 Euro per liter. So, 1,000 km will cost you around 65 Euro. Remember it.

Example:

10,000 km trip

1,000 km = 65 Euro

10,000 km = 650 Euro

= You will need 650 Euro for petrol.

10,000km: 30 days = 333km per day

333km per day. Some people will say, "Well that is easy, I can ride 1000 km. Yes, I am sure you can ride 1000 km a day. However, you cannot ride 1000 km for 30 days in a row, and if you keep in mind that during this one month period you will have at least 2 or 3 days off; all of this will reduce your average km per day. Do not forget that this is a motorcycle trip, it is not a race. Even on the famous Dakar, the guys travel between 500-800 km per day, and after two weeks they are completely exhausted.

Do you still remember that 650 Euro?

650 Euros: 30 days = 21.66 Euro

Let's just say - 22 Euro

=> You will need 22 Euro per day for petrol.

2. Accommodations

- Camping - free or paid?

Paid camping is between 10-20 Euro's per day

- Guest houses or hostels

From 10 to 30-40 Euro per day

- Hotels

From 50 all the way up to thousands of dollars.

If you want to save money:

- You will sleep mostly in your tent

15 days in the tent, 20 Euro each = 300 Euro

- If you chose wild camping - free

15 days in hotel (50 Euro room) = 750 Euro

- If you share it - 25 Euro per day. So, for 15 days it will cost you 375 Euro.

Total - 300 + 375 = 675 Euro

675: 30 days = 22,50 Euro per day

No camping, only hotels:

50 Euro room, which if you share is going to be 25 Euro.

3. Food

For food, you can easily go with 15-20 Euro per day. The price I have calculated for the food is just the basic price from buying your food and drink products from the supermarket. It doesn't mean that for 20 Euro per day, you can go to luxurious restaurants and eat to the top. This is the basic price of buying products from the supermarket and cooking them in your hostel or your camp site.

Calculations:

1. Petrol - 22 Euro per day

2. Accommodation (hotel) - 25 Euro per day

3. Food - 20 Euro per day

Subtotal - 67 Euro per day

30 x 67 euro = 2,010 Euro

Do not forget **N: 4. Unexpected costs!**

2,010 Euro + 30% unexpected = **2,613 Euro**

So, 2,613 Euro is the total price of your journey. Finally, you can see that the price for a motorcycle trip is not cheap. But this is the price for 1 month, which is not the lowest price that is possible. When I am traveling, I usually go with 50 Euro per day for Europe and about $50 per day for outside of Europe.

Of course, there are many exceptions like Scandinavian countries, because the standard there is very high, and the prices are also extremely high. The price depends on you. You are the person that decides how much you are going to spend every day. I hope this makes sense to you.

Now I am going to give you some very useful tips about how to travel as cheaply as possible.

Number 1:

Ride alone. If you ride with other people, you have to double all costs.

Number 2:

Reduce your speed. There isn't a big time difference between riding at 100 km/h and 130 km/h. But, if you are riding at 100 km/h, it will reduce your petrol consumption. For every 100 km you travel, you will save about half a litter. In a raw calculation, it is about 65 Euro for the whole trip.

Number 3:

Instead of riding with big metal cases, pack everything in a waterproof backpack and keep it behind you on the seat. Believe it or not, this will give you half a liter back for every 100 km you travel. All together with the first points, you have already saved 130 Euro. You can use this money to buy something for your wife or your kids.

Number 4:

Use a tent as much as possible or if you must, use guest houses or hostels. Over there, you will have a chance to cook your food, which will reduce the amount of money you spend out on food as well.

Number 5:

When you plan to visit big cities, do it, but go inside of the city during the early morning. Spend the whole day there, but at the end of the day, travel out of that city and find a cheaper place to sleep in. Also on the next morning, when you wake up. Staying outside of the city center will prevent you from hitting the traffic and having to wait for more than 30-40 minutes to leave that city, after just five minutes you'll be back on the open road.

Number 6:

Buy your food from a local supermarket and never from the gas station. Always keep some food with you, in case you cannot find a suitable store right away.

Number 7:

Pack as light as possible, just 2 or 3 riding t-shirts are more than enough. With light zip pants, you can go everywhere, they are so versatile. You can hike, you can go to the city, you can go to the park, you can go to the restaurant, you can go almost anywhere you want. You do not need to pack special clothes for walking around. Fewer clothes mean fewer kilograms in your bags, less overall weight on the bike results in lower consumption of fuel, and less money for laundry.

Number 8:

Use the tires which will last the longest. Believe me, in some areas the prices of tires are 3 times more expensive than the normal prices at your home.

Number 9:

Always stop on time. This will give you a chance to find a cheap place to stay. In the middle of the night when you're exhausted you'll be happy to pay any price, trust me on this one guys, I've been there already and paid the expensive prices.

Number 10:

My last advice perhaps should be the first one. Always ride safe. This will help you to avoid many unexpected costs.

******

When do you know you are ready to go on a long motorcycle trip?

I know that you expect me to give you some immediate answers, but I will surprise you and instead of answers, I have some questions for you first. Do not worry, I promise that by the end of this chapter, you will know the answer.

Today, if you just check Google, you will find tons of information and advice about how to take a long motorcycle trip. They all are very useful, no doubt, but they will not answer the question:

When are you going to be ready to do it?

Who can tell you? Everybody has a different opinion and expectations.

- How much riding experience you need to have?
- What skills do you need?

A pessimist will suggest-more experience. The optimist will say - go as soon you receive your driver license.... Who should you listen to, the optimist or the pessimist?

I will show you now a different approach. A different way to see the full picture clearly.

So, as I said in the beginning, instead of answers, you will have more questions:

1. **Plan**
- Do you have any idea where you want to go? The world is so big…
- Are prepared for that type of trip?
- Do you have a starting date?
- Do you know anything about the area you planning to visit?
- Are you going alone or in a group?
- Do you want an organized trip or just to take things day by day?

2. **Permission**

- Do you have permission to go? *From your Mother, Father, Wife, Girlfriend, Boyfriend, Family, Boss or friends.*

It sounds like something very easy to get, but actually it is not always the case, I would actually say that this is the most difficult part.

3. **Money**

- Did you sort out the financial part of the trip?
- Do you have enough money for the trip?
- Did you cover all costs while you are away? Bills, credit cards, family costs, pocket money for the kids and so on…

4. **Free time**

- Do you have enough free time?
- Can you afford to leave for a long period?
- Who will replace you? In your job, in your business? In your personal activities? In you your family bed – oops, that was a joke!

5. **Comfort zone**

- Are you ready to step out of your comfort zone?
- Are you ready to spend one day, one week, one month without your family or your friends?

- Did you accept the fact that you might not have access to the Internet, shower, proper food, a comfortable bed, television, laundry and many more things that are easily taken for granted?
- Do you know that if you travel abroad, you might not be able to stay on the telephone until you finish the free minutes you usually have?
- Are you prepared that the country you plan to go might not speak and understand your language?
- Are you aware that everything you have planned could go wrong? You can get hurt and even die?
- Did you accept the fact that at any moment, you might need to change the plan or even cancel it?
- Are you ready with some backup options?

I think that these are enough questions for now.

So, guys, when are you going to be ready for a long motorcycle trip?

Well, it is so obvious! When you have positive answers to a minimum of 90% of the questions I just asked, then, you are ready to go!

I said 90%, because you can afford to have that 10% of risk.

Ok, so now what?

Nothing, answer the questions and go ride!

******

Top 4 simple skills that you really need on a Long Motorcycle trip

Let me ask you something; what skills do you need to go on a long motorcycle trip? Well, you need riding experience, you need a lot of money, you need an expensive bike with super expensive gear, you need to have mechanical knowledge and many more things. But, is it really like that?

I will tell you exactly what I think. Let's see what the usual advice is.

Number 1:

To go on a long motorcycle trip, you need a very expensive and fancy motorcycle such as a BMW GS 1200 Adventure or similar.

Wrong! You can do it with almost any bike even with a simple 50cc scooter. Do not try to be like anyone else. You are a unique person and you can make your own journey.

Number 2:

To travel a long distance on a motorcycle, you need a lot of money.

Wrong again! You can make it really cheap or you can travel like an Arabian Sheikh. It all depends on you and your resources.

Number 3:

To protect yourself, you will need some kind of weapon, or you will need to know martial arts.

Really? I didn't know that, and I have been on so many trips. Do not even think about it and you will be fine.

Number 4:

To go on a long trip, you need very expensive gear.

Wrong! You can make a long trip with almost anything, even naked. Of course, if you have the proper gear it will be much easier, and you will be safer.

Number 5:

To go on a long motorcycle trip, you need experience.

Yes, the experience will help but tell me how all of these experienced guys started? Are they born long-distance riders, did they learn everything before they made their first trip? Of course not, the experience comes from practice. The more you travel, the more experience you will have. Do not be afraid that you will make mistakes. From your mistakes you will learn, just like I did. The fact you are reading this will already give you a head start on things.

Number 6:

To go on a long motorcycle trip, you have to know how to ride off-road.

Wrong! If your trip is only on the concrete, then you do not need it. Of course, if you have off-road skills they will help you control the motorcycle better, but it is not necessary

Number 7:

You need to know many languages.

Guys, if you know many languages yes of course they will help, but it is not a must. In the modern days, with so many technologies, we can find many easy ways to communicate with people.

Number 8:

You should know how to read maps and how to use a compass.

It is not necessary guys, you can buy very cheap and simple GPS and you will be fine. All the information will be inside. Of course, it depends on the destination but in the modern days, it is going to be very difficult to find roads without any signs. If you do find such roads do not worry, ask the locals and they will guide you.

Number 9:

To make a long motorcycle trip, you need to have very good mechanical skills, and you have to be able to fix your bike if something goes wrong.

Let's make sub topics to address this question.

- You have to be able to fix everything because when you are riding you will be on your own.

Maybe, but we can buy a brand-new bike and the problem is solved.

- You have to know how to change your tire, how to use patches for the tubes. No guys it is not necessary.

You can buy a motorcycle with tubeless tires and you can fix it very easily just with a spray or simple tools, and even if you do not want to do that, you can pay for extra assistance and call them out if something does breakdown or go wrong.

- You have to know how to change the spark plugs, how to adjust the valves, how to change the oil and many more.

As I told you guys, if you buy a brand-new bike, this problem is gone. Also, the spark plugs, the valves and the oil changes are on long intervals that you can predict it and go to the proper garages to do it when it is required. Common sense prevails, if these things are due around the time you are taking your trip, make sure they are taken care of before you go away, it's that easy.

Number 10:

To go on such a trip, you need to be in great shape. Before the trip, you need to exercise going hill climbing, swimming or whatever, and you generally need to be in the perfect shape.

Guys all of this might help if you have plans to race or enter some kind of Triathlon or you are going on some extreme ride. However, for the normal motorcycle trip, all you need to do is to change the seat of your motorcycle and ride it as often as possible. It will help you a lot more than all the activities I just mentioned.

So, with all of that being said, what exactly do you need?

You need 4 very simple things.

Number 1:

You need a motorcycle. Sounds like a very easy job but believe me it is not, ask your partner and then we will talk again.

Number 2:

You need to learn how to ride your motorcycle. It is not difficult, but you need to commit and spend time learning this. You need to be consistent and the results will come.

Number 3:

To go on a long motorcycle trip, you need free time. This is the thing that most of you guys fail to get. If you do not have free time, you can't do anything. You can do simple trips for maybe 1-2 days, but that's all.

Number 4:

At last but not at least is the will to do it. Do you have it?

******

How to get permission for your motorcycle trip?

We are men, we are bikers, but we all have one weak spot that we do not want to talk about out loud. We all dream to have an around the world trip. Probably, you will have a big world map at home. At least, I know I do. I usually look at it and dream about where my next trip will be.

I was lucky to do some very interesting trips, like Central Asia, Morocco, Norway, Alaska, Siberia Mongolia and many more. That is ok, but there is still so much to see. The world is so big. The riders from around the world, have different possibilities. Some of you, have enough money and you can ride week after week without any worry about the price of the trip. Some of you, will work very hard, to be able to save some money for the next journey.

But both trips, one with money and one without have the same important question:

"How I am going to tell my wife?"

How I am going to tell my wife or my girlfriend, that I will be gone for a month or two, because I want to go on a long motorcycle trip?

Believe me or not, this is the hardest part of the journey. I am absolutely sure that some of you guys will agree with me about that. How can I convince my wife, that it is good, it is worth it for me to go on such a trip? What I am about to tell you know is top-secret information. I hope that my wife is not reading this section!

The trick is to make it slowly, step by step, no rush. Not today, not now, not in the last minute. You have to prepare her many days or months before the trip. I will give you one example:

If I decide to go to Mongolia, I will say to my wife:

"Darling, I am going to Mongolia next month with the guys. It will take about two months."

What do you think my wife will say? Something like this:

"What? Are you crazy? You are only just telling me now? No way!"

And she will be right – no way!

Firstly, please treat your wife as you would like to be treated. Do you like nasty surprises? I guess the answer is no. So, she also be the same. If you have a plan to go on a long trip next year, now is the moment to start the preparations. The idea behind this long preparation process is that she needs time to accept it. The human brain works that way. First, we refuse something, then we see it again and again and finally you start to like it. Think about fashion, for example. The new models clothing looks strange at first, but after a few months you start to accept it. It is the same with the car industry or motorcycles. Look at the advertisement programs. They show you the same products again and again and at the end, you just buy it. We are all the same, no exceptions. This technique works without any errors. It has worked for me when I wanted to go on all my trips. I will give you a bit more detail:

For next year I have a new plan, but I started the process now:

"Honey, next year in August, I have had an idea that I want to go to Mongolia"

My wife:

"What, when, and how long for?"

Me:

"Two months, starting at the end of July or August."

She.

"No way, forget about it!"

Me:

"Ok, darling, no worries."

After one month…

"Honey, did you remember I told you about Mongolia?"

She:

"Yes, but I said no. What about it now?"

Me:

"Why not, we have to talk about it."

She:

"There is nothing to talk about, I said no. It is dangerous, and it is a long time – forget about it."

Me:

"Ok, we will talk about it later."

One more month…

Me:

"Honey, the guys are starting the preparations for Mongolia, I really want to go."

She:

"What, again! In August we usually going on holiday. It is not possible, and I am scared. It is so far away and with the motorcycles. I do not know. It is not good idea. Sorry!

Me:

"Ok, darling, but please think about it."

One more month…

Me:

"Honey, did you think any more about Mongolia?"

She:

"Yes, but my answer is still no. I told you – it is the month for the kids and is too dangerous."

Me:

"You do not need to worry about the holiday, we can go a month earlier and after we come back, I will go with the guys. Dangerous, no! Mongolia is a safe country and we are 4 people…"

She:

"I do not know, I am still worried about it. We will see. We will talk again."

Ups! We have some progress "Will talk again"! She has now started to accept the idea. Leave her for now, no rush.

After one more month…

"Darling, the time is coming, I have to prepare for the Mongolia trip. I do not want to go without your permission." - Make her feel important. "Did you think about it?"

She:

"Yes, ok. When was it, August?

Me:

"Yes. August and maybe September as well."

She:

"I am still worried about it, you will never give up, will you?

Me:

"No honey, I will not. This is my dream trip. You know I work very hard to care and look after you and the kids…"

She:

"Yes, I know, but…I will see. Are you sure that it is not dangerous?

Me:

"No, I told you it is safe, and I am not 20 years old. I have a family."

She.

"Ok, but next year we will go wherever I say!"

Me:

"Of course darling. You are a Saint! I love you so much!

So, the system works! As I said, it has worked for all my trips. It is a proven theory. It is no longer theory, it is evidence. It works with all women around the world. It doesn't matter if they are young or old, black or white, fat or slim. They all have the same brain as us. If this works for one person, it will work for all. No exceptions!

I know it takes time, but you will need that time anyway. You have to make the plans. You have to prepare the bike, to save money, to organize somebody to replace you in your job. You need to prepare some documents and so on…but you shouldn't forget your wife! Start with the permission and you will have a 100% positive answer, in the end.

******

How to choose the right motorcycle for traveling?

The ultimate adventure motorcycle, does it really exist? Here I will talk about how to choose it, what to watch out for and more.

Well, people are traveling with almost everything. From Vespa scooters to the high-end BMW R1200 GS Adventure. Sjaack Luccasen did it with a Yamaha R1, Doug's did it with his Harley, so theoretically you can do it with any bike.

The choice you have to make depends on many different variables.

- Budget
- Visual preferences
- How many km per day
- Type of riding
- The terrains you are going to ride, and many more factors

So, how do you choose the right motorcycle? Which one is the ultimate adventure machine?

A bike that is ready to go anywhere, anytime. One with a nice design, a strong engine, with very good off-road possibilities, enough luggage capacity and at an affordable price. Well my friends, I will disappoint you again!

This motorcycle doesn't exist!

As usual, now the resistance will attack me – you are not right. The **GS 1200 Adventure** is the bike!

Yes, I will agree with that statement. It is great bike, but there are only two problems with it.

1. It is bloody expensive! I have to sell my kidneys to have it.
2. It is too big and heavy! What about if you are 1.65 and weigh 70kg? The bike, with the luggage, will weight almost 3 times more.

KTM 1190 Adventure – outstanding machine. I would love to have it. But again, too expensive and very tall. For me is fine, I am about 6-foot-tall, but the price is killing me.

The new **Africa Twin** – woooow, this my dream machine, but Christmas is gone and now what? Nothing, I will wait for the next and will ask the universe to help me.

Hold on guys, it is not all bad! The ultimate adventure bike, what does it actually mean?

I will tell you how I understand it:

- You have to like this bike, do not trust the others. If you buy a bike only because somebody told you that is good and worth it, I am pretty sure you will sell it within a maximum of one year. You have your own preferences and style. Lessen yourself and go ahead. Even if you make a mistake, it will be a good experience for the future.

- It has to be easy to ride. Which means, it has to be for you. You will ride this bike, not a professional rider from Dakar Rally. If you are wondering about the ergonomics of the different models, you can go to: http://cycle-ergo.com. You can change the parameters and see how you will look on any bike

- It has to be easy to do the standard maintenance tasks. Some bikes are so complicated that even the simple things, like changing a spark plug, you have to disassemble half of the bike. Do not forget that we are talking about ultimate adventure machine, and not a motorcycle for Sunday meetings. Which means that sometimes you will face the reality and it will be in the area without any help. You have to be able to do at least the simple procedures for yourself.

- You will need a big tank. Do not focus on it so intently, 20 liters is more than enough. You have to be ready to cover at least 300 km without refueling. If it hasn't, it is not so bad either as you can even buy it later. There are many aftermarket brands like Acerbic or IMS, just keep in mind that sometimes they need some adjustment to pass through the frame of your motorcycle. I will personally suggest using tanks up to 20-22l. Bigger than that you will probably never need. If you need more, you can always buy a simple petrol can.

- Good light. Some bikes are equipped with very weak lights. On the long trip, you never know when you will need it. Even if you never ride in the dark, please make sure that your motorcycle has a proper light. Spots light and some additional gadgets I can't recommend, because your charging system might not be ready for it. You don't want to get the lights at the expense of your battery.

- Chain or drive shaft, it doesn't matter. The first is lighter, but you had to lubricate it often. The second doesn't require any maintenance on the road, but if you brake it in the middle of nowhere then it will slow your journey until you find the proper parts to fix it. So, both have some pros and cons. Belts are not recommended for adventure riding.

- Wheels. If possible choose the bike with standard sizes. 21-17 or 21-18. With these sizes, it will be easy to find proper tires. Also, with a 21inch front wheel, you will feel much better when you hit off-road sections. If the bike comes with excel rims, great. If not, you can change it later. They are stronger than stock wheels and will last much longer.

- Frame and sub frame. Adventure traveling, meaning a long trip. On such a trip, you will need a lot of things. Choose a bike with a strong frame and sub frame. We have seen enough cases of twisted and broken frames. The KTM 450 EXC is a great endurance bike, but the frame is not designed to carry 30kg of luggage on it. You have to find a solution to either make it stronger or travel lighter.

- Engine. There are many discussions about this. How big does the engine need to be? Some will say 1000CC, others will prefer 650CC. Two cylinders or thumper, it is all depends on you. Whatever suits you, your riding style and your budget. What you have to keep in mind is the oil change intervals. Some of the lighter dual-sport machines like, KTM, Husqvarna, Yamaha and many more, require oil changes at every 10 or 12 working hours. Their engine life is about 10-15,000km, after that they will need an engine overhaul. They might be great bikes, but they are not suitable for long trips.

 - Wind protection. It is something you will never think until you go on a long trip. Then you will realize just how important this is. If you have a chance to buy the one with a nice windshield then fine, if not, you can add it later. There are enough options on the net and if you do not like it, you can make your own.

- Seat. Wow.., yes, we love our butts. Tiny, narrow seats are perfect for Motocross or Enduro riding, but you will cry after 500km. Do not make this mistake. A large seat is a must. If it hasn't already got it, you can always change it later.

- Spare parts. This sounds out of place but believe me it is not. When you are choosing your motorcycle, please make sure that it is a well-known brand. Just imagine for a second that you have a breakdown situation in the middle of nowhere, and you need parts for a bike that no one has heard of. Now many Chinese companies are selling their products for very cheap prices, and it is easy to be hooked, but think twice. That is everything I can say on the matter. You have been warned!

In addition to that, what I will suggest is a light and comfortable motorcycle. The last thing you are going to need on a long motorcycle trip is a heavy bike. Yes, I will agree that sometimes the weight is a pro, but in most cases, it will be a problem. It must be suitable for the hardest part of the journey; this is how a lot of problems, energy and frustrations can be avoided.

If this is your first trip, then tried and tested one-cylinder Enduro motorcycles like the BMW Challenge, BMW Dakar, Suzuki DR, Yamaha Tenere or Honda XR are an excellent choice. Of course, everyone decides for himself how and what to travel with.

And for a final point, I would say it again: **The perfect adventure bike doesn't exist.**

Until this moment I couldn't find a model to cover everything I just said. Well, it is sounds very discouraging, but there is always hope. What I did was to buy the model which covered most of the points and then I did the rest myself. I can't push you to do the same, but at least you can think about it.

Do not forget, the bike is just a tool, the most important thing is to ride! No matter what with!

******

Top 5 Reasons to ride a Small Motorcycle on a Long Adventure trip

Most of the experienced riders will advise you that on a long motorcycle trip, you need a big adventure bike, something like a BMW GS1200, Yamaha Super Tenere or a KTM 1290 Adventure. You will need a powerful engine, big luggage capacity, and a big petrol tank is also a necessary feature, and there is nothing better than driveshaft. Yes, this is the reality, but the reality and functionality are two different things. Let me explain why:

Number 1:

The price of the trip. It is obvious that to travel the world you need a motorcycle. The big adventure bikes like a BMW GS1200, KTM 1290 or Yamaha Super Tenere will cost you no less than 15,000 Euros. When you include the price of your gear, your hard cases and many more things, the price will go up to 18,000 maybe 20,000 Euros and this will be just to have the bike, then will come the tires, oils, maintenance, taxes and insurance.

With the big bikes, the costs will be up to 50% higher compared to the prices of owning a small 600 or 650CC motorcycle. What is interesting here, is that spending that amount of money will not guarantee that you will have a better adventure, it will only guarantee that you will spend much more before you even start your trip.

Here maybe you will defend yourself and you are going to say:

"Yea but I am going to have this powerful motorcycle, I can ride up to 160km/h on the highway, and I can cover so many miles per day".

That's correct you can do it, but is this your understanding about a motorcycle adventure trip, to ride only on the highways, to sleep in luxury hotels and drink very expensive wine every night? You have to confess that the highways are boring. We do not buy motorcycles to ride on the highways, we are looking for different ways, different roads, probably twisty roads to ride and enjoy the landscape around us.

On the normal roads you can't ride faster than 120km/h which you can easily achieve with a 250CC Chinese bike. A fresh example I have is from my last trip to Russia and Mongolia. We spent almost 15,000-16,000km riding in Russia and Mongolia, but there was no highway, there were only normal roads. How fast can you ride your GS 1200 or your Ktm on these roads? They are small with a lot of traffic, so you won't be able to go faster than 120km/h. Of course, if you plan to ride only in Europe there will be 90% highways, and I perfectly understand that, but this is a different type of trip.

Number 2:

The weight. The weight always matters. If you are looking for adventure, sooner or later you will leave the comfort of asphalt roads, and you will go deep into the off-road terrain. It is just a matter of time before you realize that you have better chances to stay safe the lighter you are. With a heavy bike you have to skip some parts of the trip, or you will need help.

Number 3:

Constant speed instead of top speed. You do not need to be a mathematician to see that on a long motorcycle trip it is much better to have a constant speed instead of a top speed. You might disagree with me and say that you prefer to have a big engine and a big powerful motorcycle, but you can ride it slowly. Is that right? Why did you buy a big motorcycle then? I have seen many guys ride a small motorcycle fast, but I have never seen a guy with a big motorcycle riding slow. Actually, when I think about it I have seen some ride slow but only when they go on the dirt roads, they ride really slow, help themselves with their legs and use any kind of unusual motorcycle riding technique just to go past a simple river or a little sand.

Another con of riding fast is that you cannot really enjoy the trip because you have to be very focused on the road and your motorcycle, you cannot really look around and savor the trip. When you ride fast, you can miss important things or miss important information signs , and you increase your chances of crashing. As I said many times before it is a long motorcycle trip, it is not a race, reduce the speed if you want to see the world.

Number 4:

Less luggage. With a small and light bike you will probably go to the solution of soft luggage which is right if you ask me. By taking this decision, you will automatically reduce the number of items you take with you. You do not need to double or triple everything you will ride on Earth, not on Mars. Leave the kitchen sink and the toilet at home, they are too heavy. You might argue that on a long motorcycle trip you need more stuff, but that is not true. It is the same stuff for one week, one month, or a three-month trip. And one personal piece of advice: One month before the trip, stop going to this big motorcycle accessories shop. You will buy a lot of things you do not need. Just check what you have at home, make a list and buy exactly what you need.

Number 5:

Safety. I will split it into 2 categories: Personal and bike safety:

- **Personal safety:**

With a small and light bike, it is much easier to ride in the traffic, to make some not so legal maneuvres, to split the lanes or park the bike. It is easy to move if the engine stops working, easy to ride on and off-road, and it is easy to lift if you have to. It is more likely to stay unhurt if you fall down and get stuck under your bike. It is much easier to cross rivers or ride in the sand especially if you are alone. By having this easy control you increase the chances of finishing your trip without any problems.

- **Bike Safety**

It is much easier to find a parking spot, you can push the bike into the hotel backyards, into a small narrow street, and if you sleep in a motel on the ground floor, you can even have your bike inside your room. One very important thing is that when you have a small and cheap motorcycle, you are not attracting people who will think that you are some kind of bored millionaire and you are happy to share your wallet with everyone.

So, guys the definition of adventure is **an exciting and unusual experience** which usually involves some risk. You can do it with any bike, so instead of spending 20,000 Euro for a motorcycle, spend 5,000-7,000 and use the rest to see the world.

******

Oversize tank or simple petrol can – which one is better?

The Oversize tank or a petrol can, which one is better for a long motorcycle trip? Let's make it clear right from the beginning, for an oversize tank I will specify any tank above 20l, because it is obvious that with 10l on the motorcycle, it will be difficult to travel.

So, which one is best?

As you already know, in the last 10 years the big adventure motorcycles have become very popular. The GS 1200, Yamaha Super Tenere, KTM 1090, 1290, Triumph Tiger and many more. This new fashion went around the world, spraying the message that it is almost impossible to make an adventure trip if you do not have one of the models I just said. They went even further by adding huge petrol tanks of 25, 27 and even 30l to some of the models. The idea behind this, is that when you go to really wild and remote areas, without petrol stations around, you can have this huge 500 or 600km range and you do not need to worry about anything. That's right, but like many other ideas, it is only good on paper, let me explain why:

First and most importantly, it is very difficult today, in 2018 to find places around the world, with so many km without any petrol station. Now, as usual, the resistance will attack me, no, you are not right, in Central Asia, in South America, in the African desert or Australia you can find many places like that.

I was in Central Asia, 3 years ago and the longest destination without a petrol station was 450km, but they were working on the new road there, which means that there will now be petrol stations. South America, I hope to go there next year, but I am sure that the reality is very similar or better.

What about Africa or Australia? There are millions of people who live there driving cars or riding motorcycles, do you think that they all fill their tanks once every 500 or 600km? This is just not real.

What I am basically trying to say is that there will be more than enough solutions to fill your tank and you do not really need to worry about it so much. It might be just a simple barrel and local guy, but you will find petrol.

Of course, the resistance never gives up:

What about the desert, Australian outback or somewhere in the mountains? There are no roads there, how are you going to find a petrol station?

Guys, how many of you ride big Adventure bikes in these areas? Let's be honest and confess that any bike above 200kg, include the luggage will be way too heavy on such a trip. How many GS 1200 Adventure owners you have met in the desert, in the mountains or in the bush? It is absolute nonsense! Everyone, who ever tried to ride a motorcycle off-road, knows that the weight is always important.

Did you remember the great movie 'Long Way Round', with Ewan McGregor and Charlie Boorman, with their 300kg BMW GS 1150 Adventure? I am sure you do. It is a great movie, great riders, but they had a large support team and could have done it much easier if they had lighter bikes, especially in Siberia and Mongolia.

To make the long conversation short – on the wild and remote adventure trip, without possibility to refill your tank, you should go with as light a motorcycle as possible. The big adventure bikes with huge 30l petrol tanks are nothing but more than a useless piece of metal.

Well, this chapter supposes to be for petrol tanks and cans, and I convert it to the forever battle big vs small motorcycles, sorry about that! Let's see the pros and the cons of each one of the options.

I will start with the big petrol tanks.

Pros:

- A big petrol tank will give you a huge range of independence, 500, 600 or 700km. I will add one question mark here, because this is valid only if you travel alone. If you are in a group, your independence is limited to the range of the smallest tank in the group.
- You can avoid some problems coming from bad petrol. For example, if the petrol in a certain area is of very low quality.
- You can help a friend on the road if they run out of petrol.
- You can save some money if you fill the tank in the countries with cheaper petrol.

Cons:

- Big tanks are equal to more weight. As I said hundreds of times, the weight always matters. Even if you keep your tank half empty, you still will have additional 5 or 7 kg of extra weight because of the tank itself. If you keep it empty most of the time, this only means that you do not really need it.
- Most of the aftermarket solutions are not cheap. The price range is between $300-$500.
- Some of the brands cannot be mounted properly. You will need an additional hardware or adjustments to the existing machine. This could cause many problems during your trip. Especially if you plan a lot of off-road.
- Because they are not designed exactly for the models, you might have difficulties to access your engine components like spark plugs or cables.
- Sometimes they cannot be drained properly and always have some litter inside.
- For fuel injection models, it is difficult to find a solution, because usually the fuel pump is mounted in the tank.

The simple solution for all of the problems I just discussed here is to get a motorcycle that is as light as possible. If the tank is not that big, you can easily carry extra petrol with you. You can find so many different options today. From a simple petrol can, to any kind of useful solutions that help you to carry extra fuel.

Petrol cans Pros:

- They are very cheap, and you can buy them from everywhere.
- They are light, no more than 2kg empty.
- You can buy it and fill it only when you need it.
- Because of the cheaper price you can leave it, when you do not need it.
- Easy to add petrol in yours or your friends tank.
- It could be used not only for petrol, you can fill it up with water, or with handmade alcohol, like my friend Dima. Just make sure that you wash it properly or use it for water first and later for petrol, otherwise you going to have this strange taste all the time.

Let's talk about cons:

- You have to find a place to mount it. It could be your tail, passenger pegs or sides. It is easy when it is empty, but different when it is full.
- You risk a bit because it could be spill over your bike or get burned from the exhaust if it is not mounted on the right place.

I cannot really remember any other cons, let me know if you know some.

So, with just a few words, stop worrying about the size of the tanks. 20 or 22 liters are more than you will ever need today. If you really plan to travel in such a terrain, instead of spending 5,000 Dollars more for an expensive super adventure bike, the same as yours, but with a bigger tank, buy a simple petrol can for 5 Dollars and the problem is solved.

******

Top 5 Myths about Motorcycle Auxiliary Lights

We all know just how important visibility is to motorcyclists and because of that, many of you will start to think about or may have even already bought auxiliary lights (also known as spot or adventures lights). Many of you will truly believe that they are absolutely necessary, especially for a long-distance type of trip. As usual, I am here to question this theory and bust the top 5 myths about auxiliary lights.

I am aware that what I just said could generate a huge debate on this topic. Many of you will dislike what I am saying. However, I truly believe that if you listen with an open mind, and ignore the fact that you may have already spent money on these fancy looking adventure lights, you will be able at least to see one alternative opinion.

Myth N: 1 - They are absolutely necessary

The presumption has almost always been that they are completely necessary if you plan a long trip and have plans to ride in the dark. The idea is to have better visibility and prevent collisions with other moving objects, like cars, animals or maybe even to help you avoid potholes on the road. Ok, it makes perfect sense. However, could you please explain to me why some of the most famous motorcycles for long trips, the best-known cruisers do not have or need auxiliary lights?

The Honda Goldwing, BMW K 1600, Ducati Multistrada and even the BMW 1200 GS. These bikes are designed to spend thousands of miles on the roads. How are they going to do it without these fancy additional lights?

I see, because they have very good stock lights - fair enough. As far I know the BMW 1200 GS also has excellent lights, am I right? Headlights, high beam even modern LED lights. So because of that, there is no need for any additional lighting. That is right, and they do not have it, as you can see in the picture, but on the Adventure models, they add it. Why?

Aha, now I understand. Now it is become perfectly clear to me: Because it is an adventure bike and you cannot go on adventure trip without such lights!

Really, I did not know that, and because of my stupidity, I have done thousands of km around the world without it. What ignorance! And I call myself adventure rider and I do not have adventure lights, how that is even possible?

Because I follow the normal and simple logic – no light, no ride!

Let me explain to you what exactly I mean. On long trips, I spend many hours in the saddle. Every day, I ride between 300-1,000km. If I am strict and everything is going well, this tempo will give me everything I need to complete my trip. Why the hell do I need to ride at night?

If you are a post courier or pizza delivery and spend many hours riding in the night, I understand. Not completely, because in the cities these lights are useless, but I almost can understand where you are coming from.

If you have to commute between towns and you start at 03:00 in the morning, I understand. You do need some extra lights, but on the long trips – I am sorry, I still cannot see any benefits from it, maybe I am stupid! Or perhaps people just pay all this extra money for these lights because they think they look good? Who knows.

Now the main argument against me will be – No No No, you are not right. From a safety perspective, you should have these lights. More lights equal better visibility – it is so obvious! How you cannot see it?

Well, it looks like I am not alone, as I already said, Honda, Yamaha, Suzuki, BMW, Ducati and many more didn't see it as well, that is unless you buy an adventure model. Then becomes different, and you will definitely need it.

So on the normal models, the safety is not important. Is that is what we have to believe? Is there any logic to this?

Yes, because long-distance/adventure trips are different from the normal trip. Really, what is the difference? Maybe it is because on a normal trip you will only ever ride in perfect conditions, no fog, no dark, no rain, just sunshine and great roads. On the other hand, on an adventure trip, you never know what you are going to face. You have to be prepared for everything!

I told you I never give up, so tell me the biggest adventure as I know it is the Dakar Rally. You know the guys there need to face some of the most extreme terrains and riding conditions on the planet. Now tell me, have you ever seen a Dakar bike with additional lights? Does this mean something to you?

Yes, but there is a very simple explanation for this, they always try to save weight. These are race bikes. Aha, but they have already added so many heavy things, such as a road book, Sentinel, GPS, Iritrack and many more. Actually, every bike is equipped with about 2kg of additional stuff in the name of safety, but they miss the simple spotlights, how?

Although we could continue conversations like this forever; I think that I have said enough and you already understand what I mean. Whether or not you agree, I think I have made my point here.

Myth N: 2 – They will not harm your electric system.

The Stator or the Alternator of any bike is designed to produce enough electricity exactly for the specific model. If you plug in some additional lights, then you have to be very careful of exactly how much electricity they will consume. The end result if you do not do this could mean you need to replace the battery.

The second big risk to consider is the possible circuit or bad connections that could be caused by poor or cheap installation.

Myth N: 3 – They are safe to use all the time.

This statement is not correct. In many countries, it is only possible to use additional fog lights when the weather is bad, such as during heavy rain or fog. Also, the chances of blinding the oncoming traffic are very big, especially in the dark. The stock lights are properly designed to prevent this from happening, and that is exactly why we have a head light and high beam. However, with auxiliary lights you have one light spread to all sides.

Myth N: 4 – They will give you the filling light you need.

Is more light equal to more safety? Maybe, but I cannot agree 100% with this statement. The most dangerous part of riding in the night comes from the objects in front of you. The faster you ride, the faster they come, and the less time you will have for a reaction. The additional lights usually give more filling light, but on both sides of the bike, not in front of the bike, and definitely not from 30m ahead. I know there will be some people who will say, yes, but it will be very useful if an animal comes from the side. Yes, they could be, but you only will see it in the last few meters when it comes to the illuminated part, and I think that it will be too late for any reaction. If safety is your main concern, just don't ride at night.

Myth N: 5 – They will increase your visibility.

I partly agree with this, but not the level to get one for myself. As I told you, I have spent thousands of km without it, and I have no problems with visibility. I think that it will be much more beneficial for you to learn how to ride properly to increase your visibility. For example, sometimes I ride on high beam, only during the day, to be visible from a longer distance away. Also, I never make maneuvers before I am 100% certain that everybody in the traffic knowss that I am there. With most of the bikes, the head light is always on, and nearly all new models now come with extra LED day lights which have this really bright light; I think that this is more than enough. I suggest buying a helmet in white or some reflective color as it will help you much more than you can imagine. So if your main concern is safety, I go back to my earlier suggestion that you never ride in the dark, and you will increase your chances to stay alive probably by at least 500%.

Hard vs Soft Luggage - Which is better?

So, which one is better? To have a nice, expensive hard case system or cheap saddlebags.

I am so glad that you expect me to tell you the magic formula, but I will disappoint you and tell you it does not exist. It all depends on many circumstances. For example, riding alone or with people, how long is the ride going to be. What are your preferences, how much luggage are you going to take, how much does your luggage weigh etc. As I said at the beginning, I do not have this universal answer, but I will tell you what I think.

I prefer soft luggage saddle bags or a big waterproof bag, whatever is better for the trip I plan. I'm absolutely sure that now at this moment some of you guys will disagree with my statement and you will attack me with some very strong arguments.

Number 1

Security. If you have hard cases, you can lock your stuff on the bike and you do not have to worry about it when you walk around. That's correct, but do you know how simple the locks of your side cases are. They look like the ones on my post-box, but because of that, it doesn't matter how simple it is, it will be more common to leave your bike in the not so good locations and you leave it for a longer period because you believe that this lock will save your luggage. An average Steve will steal your bike in less than 10 seconds. He will just break your ignition system or your bars lock and will steal your bike that fast.. Just keep this in mind. Your ignition system key or your steering lock system is much stronger and much more difficult to break, than the locks you have on your saddle bags. So how much time do you think the thief will need to open your side cases? The answer is not much. On the other hand, if you have soft luggage, you have to find a solution to park your motorcycle in a better position, maybe in front of a café or you will ask somebody else to take care of your bike, you will lock it with the cable with the pack safe mesh.

Number 2

The hard cases are waterproof. That's correct, but it depends on the model. I have seen hard cases full of water after just simple rain and I have seen a lot of saddlebags or what waterproof bags untouched and completely dry after a whole day of rain, so it really depends on the model. You get what you pay for so investing in a robust solution is important.

Number 3

You can have more luggage in it. I will disagree with that. Yes, when you have hard cases, it usually means you can take more stuff, but do you really need that stuff? The reality is that the hard cases are very limited, so you have this square space and inside you can put 35 litters, 42 litters or 50 litters. It depends on the size of your case, but you can't put more in. On the other hand, when you have a saddlebag with 35 litters, you can put in a little bit more because you can extend it on the side, so you can put something else inside. What usually happens is that people mount the hard cases system, they fit it in and then on top of the cases they put soft cases and one big waterproof bag, this only results in more luggage. But it is not because your hard case system allowed you to put more in, it is because you have found this different solution to take more luggage with you.

Number 4

f you have a hard case system, you can load heavier stuff in. That's correct, but do you think this is a plus? I personally think that this is a big minus. You shouldn't take too much stuff with you. You're not with a car, you're with motorcycle. Any weight matters. When you use a hard case system, you usually will overload your motorcycle and you will take the stuff which is not needed.

Number 5

With hard cases, you'll have a lower centre of gravity. Well, yes and no. If you have a nice brand, a proper mounting system, if you load it right, yes, you can have lower centre of gravity, but in most cases, it is the opposite. In fact, with a nice saddlebag system, you can have much better result. First because it is lighter and second because you can find a better position because they are not fixed as suitcases. You can move it to the right or to the left until you find a perfect position for your saddlebags.

Number 6

You can store your food better. Correct, but it will be much better if you take your fridge, then your beer will always be cold, and you will have everything nearby. Are you going on a motorcycle trip, or to a culinary journey?

Number 7

It looks better. Really, you think these square boxes look better on your bike? I cannot agree with this. Sorry. Is this enough or do you want me to keep going?

We just finished with the pros of the hard luggage system, let's talk about the cons.

Number 1

First and the most important is the weight. Hard cases with a mounting system are the best scenario, weighing about 10 kg. Ten extra kilograms before you have even started to load it. When you're riding a motorcycle, sooner or later you will find out that weight is a problem, it will be when you need to load your bike or when you drop off your bike and you have to take out all the cases just to lift the bike and then load it again or when you're stuck somewhere in the mud or in the sand, it doesn't matter. I'm sure at some stage you will agree with me and you will remember my words.

Number 2

Safety if you fall down as both you and you're riding partner will have a serious risk of getting hurt. I have seen enough situations whereby hard cases hurt people's legs or in some situation even break them, especially if you have big metal cases with sharp edges, so it is a real danger.

Number 3

Overloading. Because of the possible overloading, you risk bending your frame or your sub frame or even cracking it. This happens all the time, you can search the internet and find thousands of situations of people overloading their bikes and the frame or sub frame getting cracked or damaged. When you're, for example, in the middle of nowhere where are you going to find a welder to fix your frame? I think it is going to be much, much easier to find a solution to fix a hole in your saddlebag than to try and find somebody to weld your frame or sub-frame. This kind of thing can really set you back and ruin your long-distance adventure.

Number 4

Price. Have I told you that a nice brand of a hard case with a mounting system costs about $500, $600 up to $800? I should have started with this, I guess.

Number five.

Petrol consumption. When you're riding with big cases on the side, your engine uses about half a liter more petrol per each 100 kilometres. On a 10,000 kilometres trip, it will cost you about 60-70 Euro more. When we have a strong wind, these cases turn into a sail and you have a higher petrol consumption. So, at the end of the journey I am sure you would have spent more than 100 Euro or more just because of the side cases. Believe or not, it has already been tested many times. I honestly cannot find any benefits to having a hard case system on my bike.

Sorry, there is one. You can add a lot of travel stickers around your side cases from around the world, all the places you have been, and then in this situation you will look like a real great adventurer.

******

How to prepare your Motorcycle for a long trip?

How should you prepare your motorcycle so as not to face problems along the way?

I do not know where you will be travelling, or if it will be on good or bad quality roads. Will it be on the highways around the big cities or in remote areas? With the first option, spare parts and mechanic shops you can find easily, but with the second they are a luxury that is completely out of the question.

Naturally, I believe that one can get help everywhere but, in any case, it is better to be prepared. So, how can you prepare for everything that could occur and make sure you have everything you might need?

The answer is quite simple – there is no way to do that. The best approach is to change everything that is due to be changed or it will need to be performed soon enough:

A list of some of the parts you might have to change or least check

- Bearings front and rear wheels, bearings on the suspension and triple clamp as well.
- Checking the seals on the forks and change the oil if necessary.
- Brake pads, front and rear. Rotors – if they are due for a change, do it.
- New chain with sprockets. If the bike is with drive shaft – inspect it.
- New tires
- Regulating Valves

- Oil and filters, naturally this is beyond doubt. New spark plug/s depending on the cylinders.

All of these (without the tires) is better if it is tested before the actual departure so that you can be sure that everything is in place and it works correctly.

Spare Parts

Due to the lack of luggage space, you must take with you only the absolute necessities:

- Clutch and brake levers
- A spare relay regulator. Adding a voltmeter to the dash will help you catch it in time if there's a problem with the relay.
- A unit chain, even two – they do not weigh much at all and they can save you a lot of problems
- A spare clutch cable. I personally tied it with tie wraps to the other one, that way I do not have to carry it and what's more important is to have it go under the reservoir. It is a slow and trying procedure, even more so if you are in a hurry or if it is dark, cold etc.
- Spark plug
- A few meters of cable
- Spare brake pads
- Nuts and bolts of the most common type on the bike. Tie wraps/zip ties and wire
- A spare tire, a set of instruments for repair work must always accompany the motorcycle.

******

Long Motorcycle Trip - Alone or in a group?

How to ride on a long motorcycle trip. Alone or in a group?

Everything I am going to tell you is what I think. It is all based on my experience and I don't have any goals to teach you or to change the opinion you already have.

Let's start with riding a group.

Pros:

Number 1

It is good to be part of a large group. We are humans and we love this feeling, you can check on Facebook and you will be amazed at how many groups you will find there.

Number 2

The group will give you some confidence and safety, especially if you are a new rider. There will be more than enough experienced people ready to help you.

Number 3

Personal and bike safety. You don't need to worry about anything because there will always be somebody who will look after you or your bike. It is easy to receive any help if you need it.

Number 4

Possibilities to learn a lot. From simple riding techniques to very useful tricks about how to ride a motorcycle. Also, you will have the chance to build very strong friendships. As you know, we are all like brothers, when we pass each other we shake hands.

Number 5

Discounts and fun. You will have a chance to receive many discounts because you are a large group and also you will have a good amount of fun when you join at a restaurant or a bar.

Number 6

Easy logistics. Somebody will do it for you and you don't need to worry about anything, just ride your motorcycle.

Those are all of the pros, now we will talk about the cons.

Number 1

Timing. You will move much slower. Even if you ride fast, you will move slowly. I will explain why. Every person is different - some wake up early, and some don't. Some prefer to drink coffee, some don't. Some will go to the toilet early in the morning, some will go during the trip and so on. All of this will slow down your start. If you have plans to start at 7:00 in the morning, you will actually start at 8:00 or 8:30.

Number 2

Confrontations. You will have confrontations, different bikes, different people, and different riding styles. Stopping once every 15 minutes, once per hour or never stopping. Everybody will ask for something different, even if you agree before that, that you are going to stop every two hours, the differences will start as soon as you hit the road. Some will prefer to drink a coffee at every stop, some will prefer to have a nice lunch and so on. When many people are involved, it is almost impossible to have strict timing and the confrontations will follow.

Number 3

Dangerous riding and imitations. Some experienced riders, usually the leaders will ride fast or we'll use some techniques to impress the rest of the group, especially the new riders. They can afford it because they know what they are doing, but it's just not like that for the newbie riders behind. They will try to do the same. Taking a serious risk to have an accident or even to die

Number 4

Accommodation problems. Some people prefer nice hotels, some prefer to tent. It all depends on the budget you have for your trip. At the end you have to make a lot of compromises. It is easy to find rooms for two or three people. But it's a different story when you are 5, 6, 10, or more. Even in the camping areas it could be a problem, especially when you're hitting a high season.

Number 5

Logistics. You may not agree with some of the roads or some of the directions, but you're in a group.

Number 6

High cost. It will cost you more because of everything that I just described in the previous five points, at the end, you will spend much more money if alone.

Let's see, what is the situation when you're riding alone? **Pros:**

Number 1

Riding style. You're the boss. Ride as long as you need, stop when you decide, drink when you're thirsty and eat when you're hungry.

Number 2

It is easy to find a place to sleep. Cheaper prices and very good chances to be invited into people's homes, the choice is yours.

Number 3

Easy logistics. You can choose all the destinations, all the attractions, everything you want to see, it's your choice, and you're the boss.

Number 4

It is cheaper. You are the boss. You control your budget. If you want to travel cheap you can. It's your decision.

Number 5

Communication. You don't need to talk with anyone when you travel alone. You can spend the whole journey in silence. It all depends on you.

Let's see the cons:

Number 1

No help when you need it. If you're in the city or on the main roads somebody will help you, but if you're far away from civilization, somewhere in the middle of nowhere, it will be difficult and almost impossible to find somebody to help you. So, you have to be ready and you have to be prepared for anything that could possibly happen to you. Even the small things like a flat tire or an empty tank could be a real, real problem during that time.

Number 2

Loneliness. Some people feel really bad when they're left alone. If you're that type of person it could be a disaster.

Number 3

Security. You have to look after your bike and your stuff all of the time when you travel. Even the simple things like going to the gas station or across the street to check for free room in a hotel is a problem because you cannot just leave your bike with everything on it.

Number 4

Personal safety. Alone, you're an easy target.

Number 5

Dangerous. I will not recommend you to go on a long motorcycle trip alone, especially if you have plans to go to an area with no people or off-road. I will tell you one personal story. I love to ride off-road, I used to do it before, I started in a group, but I soon realized that riding in this group and climbing hills, digging in deep river beds and trying any kind of possible way to destroy my motorcycle was not my passion, so I started riding alone.

I did it for a couple of years without any problems. Then once, when I was riding somewhere in the middle of the forest and I just missed one corner, I fell in big hole next to the road. It was not that bad, I was not hurt thanks to the gear, but I needed to take my bike out of the hole. It was not that deep, maybe a meter and a half. But it was difficult to get it back out and I tried to keep in mind that this bike was only 120 kilograms. So I spent almost 30 minutes trying to take my bike out. I was totally exhausted when I did it and as soon as I did it, I saw that my rear tire was flat. I had no tools, no spare tube, I had nothing. I can use my telephone to call somebody, but I cannot describe where I am because usually when I'm riding I never check the roads. So I don't know where exactly I am. I have an idea where I am, but not exactly the point, so if I call somebody to help, I can't clearly describe to them where I am. He could spend all day looking for me without any results.

So, I decided to ride my motorcycle with the flat tire, and I did it. Then, the next problem was that I was about 50 kilometers away from my hometown, so I rode these 50 kilometers at about 10 km/h on the side of the road, very slowly and every car which was going around me was stopping and telling me that my tire was flat. I don't know what the people were thinking, but I'm not a truck with 16 tires. I have only two tires. Of course, I know my tire is flat. So anyway, when I get home I had to buy a new tire, a new tube, and a new wheel because mine was bent so I had to replace it all. All of these could have been avoided if I had a friend with me. He could have just taken my tire went to the shop and fixed it for me. This was funny, but what about if I was seriously injured? What about if I had a broken leg or something more dangerous? So think about it.

Riding alone or in a group?

The question is still there. I don't know the answer, but I will tell you what I would do.

The magic number is two. Yes, two people. Find a friend to ride with you. Someone who has a similar bike as yours that has the same riding style, you will share the same passion, someone with a budget that is the same as yours. Chose the destination, agree about the roles and enjoy your trip.

Of course you will have to make some compromises, but believe me, they are nothing compared to the other two options I just described and don't forget, it doesn't matter with whom, where, or with what, the most important is to ride.

Simple Maintenance for Long Motorcycle trips

Now I'm going to tell you what you have to do before your long motorcycle trip. When I say long, I mean 10,000 kilometers or more. If you have an unlimited budget, this is not for you, but if you're willing to do it as cheap as possible, then read on.

The easiest way to do it is to drop the bike in the local garage and get them to do it for you. That's okay, but here in Germany, this procedure will cost me thousands of Euros. It is a lot of money. Actually, this is half of my budget for my next long trip. I know what you're going to say now: "It's easy for you, but I don't know anything about it" Just calm down. You don't need to be a mechanic to do some kind of a 'do it yourself' maintenance. Most of the things I'm going to tell you are very easy to do if you just check your manual.

First step guys, is to lift the bike from the ground. You can use your central stand or a jack. Inspect your brake pads and the rotor. If they're in the middle of their life, change them. Of course, it is the same for the rear. Just keep in mind that the best option is to change the brake pads and rotors at the same time. This will provide you with the maximum mileage after that. Usually, it's a very simple, procedure and you can do for yourself if you just check your manual.

Check the condition of your front wheel bearing by spinning the tire around and listening for a strange noise or maybe the best option is to grab the wheel and try to move it from one side to another. If you feel even a simple movement, this means you have to change it as soon as possible. Repeat the same process with your rear wheel.

Check and if necessary, change the bearings on the steering column as well. You can make this change by simply moving the forks from left to right and listening for strange noises or some kind of vibrations. Of course, the best option is to remove the forks and leave the tripod clamp just to move freely without any weight on it. Then you can see it much easier.

If you don't have a brand-new bike or you have never changed the bearings on your bike, I would recommend you to do it before the trip. If you do so, this can prevent many problems, and you can save a lot of time and money or your next trip.

The next step is to check your chain and sprockets. If they show some kind of indication of wearing, just change them. They might look fine, but if you have more than 20,000 kilometers on them, it doesn't matter, just change them. It is very important to change the chain and sprockets at the same time. This will secure a maximum mileage after that. If you have a drive shaft, check the oil level and inspect for leaking. Inspect your throttle cables. They need to move freely without any holds or noises. It is the same with your clutch cable. Just check it for rust or some kind of rigid movements. If you have a hydraulic probe, then check the oil level. Of course, check the oil level of the brakes as well.

Your electrical system is a very important part of your motorcycle. Make sure that all the cables are fine and ensure that connections are clean. If necessary, remove the tank or sweep the bike completely to check all of the cables. In some places, the cables connect to the frame, so they actually touch the frame. When you move your steering from left to right all the time, these cables always touch the frame, and throughout this, they can cause damage the cover of your cables. Make sure that you check all of that because it could be a real problem, it could even cause a fire. Of course, check all of your lights, headlights, high beam, indicators, and flashlight. Go to the back and check the brake lights, the stoplight check, and even the light for your number plates. All of this is very, very important.

The next very important step is the oil change. Of course, change the oil filter and the air filter as well. Inspect the antifreeze level and the condition, if its dirty then change it, of course, inspect it for some kind of leaking. If you have an air-cooled motorcycle, just inspect the metal elements of the cylinder and the cylinder head.

Change the spark plug, and if you have more than one, change them all. Usually the sparks last about 10,000 kilometers, so if you're half on the waymark then just change it. You can keep it as a spare in your luggage. It is better to do it now rather than later on the road. In some bikes, the access to the spark plug is so difficult that actually, you have to strip back half of the bike to get access to it. Inspect the frame and the sub frame for cracks and damages, if you find some or if you have plans to load a lot of luggage, make sure that you reinforce it properly.

Buy new tires and new tubes. You can find very cheap tires and tubes on eBay, but I would recommend you to do it in the local garage. Yes, it will cost you more, but you will have a fresh tire, they will do it properly and also they will balance the wheel, and if you're lucky, you will come back without any punctures. If you want to save some money, remove the wheels from your motorcycles and bring them to the garage, this will reduce the price significantly.

Another very simple but very important step is to lubricate all of your locks. For this, you can use chain spray. Just spray a little bit inside and then put your key in and move it left and right a couple of times and repeat the process with all the locks you have on the motorcycle. Over the years of use, a lot of dust comes inside, and sometimes the locks just get stuck. It will be very bad if gets stuck in the middle of nowhere.

Now, guys, we're coming to the difficult part or the part where you will need help or some mechanical skills. Checking the valve clearance. It is not that difficult of a procedure. Usually, it is explained very well in your manual, but if you don't want to do it, just go to a local garage. On some bikes like a BMW boxer, for example, it's a very easy procedure. You can just remove the cylinder heads covers, and this makes it so easy, but on my bike, for example, I need more than three hours. The actual process of adjusting the valves takes 15 minutes, but I need more than two hours to remove the tank, the seat, etc. One possible option is to go to the local garage and ask the guys there if somebody will want to come to your home and do it for you, then you can do the hardest part of stripping the bike and just leave the mechanic to finish the other part for you. Then you can save some money.

The next step is the forks and shock inspection. It is not that difficult of a process, but you have to have special tools to do it. And usually, these tools cost about 100 Euros. So, for about the same money or a little bit more, I will go to the local garage and they will do it for me. Of course, to save money, I will remove the forks from the motorcycle and just bring them to the garage and then they will reduce the price by maybe half.

Removing the forks from the motorcycle is not that difficult. It is almost the same on any bike, of course with small differences. First, you have to remove your wheel then you unscrew the bolts, and you can easily twist and remove the forks. Usually, you will have a few bolts on top of the triple clamp, and the same number of bolts on the bottom of the triple clamp.

Don't forget to check the linkage and the bones underneath. Lubricate or if necessary, change them.

After you do all of these guys, you're ready to go. It is impossible to predict everything, but at least we can try to deal with everything that is within our control before setting off on a long-distance motorcycle trip.

******

How to Protect yourself and avoid problems on a Long Motorcycle Trip

It can sound quite scary to travel with a motorcycle in a different country, especially if you know nothing about it. The news today makes it even worse, representing the world as such a dangerous place and frightening us with any kind of possible problems or wars. It looks like that if you try to do it, you'll be in danger, and you might be hurt or even die. As usual, I will try to convince you that it's not exactly like that and will give you 10, very useful tips, how to protect yourself.

Number 1

Change your perspective. Change the way you see the world. If you think that, to travel with a motorcycle is a dangerous hobby. Guess what? You're right. On the other hand, if you think that when you travel, you're going to meet only nice, happy people. You're right, again. I know that it sounds very confusing but let me explain this to you.

As you already know, I love examples, and I have another one for you. It's a bit of long story, but please be patient and stay with me until the end because this is the best advice I can give you to help protect yourself. When I was 20 years old, I was a very aggressive person, and out of the seven days of the week, I was fighting probably 10 times. I was fighting for everything, for respect, for my friends, for girls, for my rights, for any reason you can imagine. My mother and later my wife always told me that if I keep fighting, then sooner or later, somebody will kill me. At that time, I really believed that the world was a dangerous place and the only way to survive was to use my fists. One day, I met a friend of mine, a very nice educated guy who was never a part of the life I had. He had just gotten a piercing on his eyebrow.

Being from the old school, my first reaction was: "Man, what the fuck is this? What have you done? If somebody punches you in the face, you can lose half of your eyebrow or lose your eye. Why did you do it?" He looked at me surprised and said: "Why would someone want to punch me? I tried to explain it to him that usually when the people fight, they punch each other in the face or in the body. He was even more confused and replied: "Why should I fight with someone? Is this the only way? Is this the only solution?" I couldn't really understand his reaction, and I insisted because sooner or later it will happen. 'It's never happened to me, and I don't think that it ever will,' was his answer and then I realized that he was right. He has a different perspective, a different way to see the world and his life was different. This was the first time when I started to doubt this direction. Of course, it took some time to convince myself and to change my life, but finally about 15 years ago, I completely changed my life and the way I see the world. Since then, I have never had to fight, and I never had such a problem. I had other problems, but not those kind of problems.

I know for many of you guys, it will be very hard to accept it. That's why I have the rest of the tips, but don't forget this is the most important one I can give you. Change the way you see the world and the world will change for you.

Number 2

Information. As you know, in the modern day, it's everything. Forget about television and newspapers and find a trustworthy source of information. Read books, real stories, watch videos about the place. Find people who've been there and talk with them. Learn about different cultures and traditions. Learn what the proper way to behave in that country is.

Number 3

Religion. Respect their religion and don't flag with yours. Don't try to teach, judge or change them. As I said many times, some things cannot be changed. Stop to believing that your country or your religion is the best of the world and everybody needs to bend knees in front of you. Remember, you are not God, you're not the sun, and you're just a guy with a motorcycle who wants to see their country. You are a visitor, you're a guest in their home, please behave as a guest should.

Number 4

Avoid big cities. Yes, if it's possible, avoid the big cities. Spend the night in a village or a small town nearby. It will save you a lot of money and many possible problems. Over there, you will find much cheaper hotels, and usually, the people in smaller communities are friendlier and more open-minded.

Another good reason to do it is that on the next morning, instead of spending one or two hours in traffic in 15 minutes time, you'll be ready to go. I'm not telling you that you have to skip all big cities. I know that some of the big cities are very interesting, and you have to see them. What I am saying is just to have a hotel in a village nearby and go to visit the city and come back to your hotel.

Number 5

Don't drink with the locals. As you know, alcohol gives you some courage and even a calm and peaceful person could become a menace. You can do it only if you have friends there if they invite you to their home or with their friends or something like that. For example, now on our trip to Mongolia, our Russian friends told us that the last thing and the worst thing you can make in Mongolia is to try to drink with Mongolians. They become very aggressive, they all have knives, and it could become a real problem from nothing.

Number 6

Hotels. Always choose a normal, not expensive hotel. You don't need to show that you're one of those rich guys. Don't look like a fish, ready to be eaten, be friendly with locals and do not tell them more than they should know about you.

Number 7

Money. Be careful with your cash and keep as little as possible with you. Credit cards mean nothing in some countries, but the cash could be a huge temptation, that some people cannot resist. By showing your cash in public places, like restaurants, bars or shops. You increase the chances of being attacked or robbed. Dima for example is not very careful. Sorry, my friend but I have to tell them, as I really believe that it could help someone. Sorry, once again.

So, usually, when he needs to pay for something that's $10-$20, he takes out all of his money, $1000 or $2,000 and tries to find a $10 note. But, one time, while searching for 10$, he spilled all his money everywhere. It became like a shower of money, and then he had problems collecting and keeping all he money back while the people were watching. Don't make the same mistake as Dima. It's like a gamble with your luck. Keep your money in at least two different places. Keep in your pocket only the money you're going to need for that day. The rest, you need to hide somewhere in your cloak, in your baggage, in your motorcycle, I don't know, but in your pocket, keep only the amount you're going to need on the day.

Number 8

Weapons. If you carry a knife or ax, for example, hide it somewhere. Some people might be very upset if they see it. In fact, pepper spray will help you much more than you can imagine, but of course, it's your decision. Remember that taking out your knife or your ax should be your last possible option, before that you have to find any kind of possibility to calm down the situation and make it peaceful. If you cannot, make it fast, and try to escape as soon as possible from the place before the whole village comes to you.

Number 9

Spot tracker device. If you really worry about your safety, I highly recommend that you take one of these devices. It will track you all the time, and your friends and your family will know where exactly you are every minute. In case of a problem, they will know, and they will send a text message, or you can even press the help button, and you shall receive help as soon as possible. Keep in mind that the coin has two sides. Sometimes the GPS signal is weak, or the battery dies, and it will not show properly what's going on so you have friends at home who are looking at the computer will start to call you: "What's going on? Why are you not moving? Is there any problem? Are you stuck or something like that?"

Number 10

People are good. Please remember that phrase. I know it's hard to believe, but this is the best way to protect yourself. Instead of seeing an enemy and threat in every person, focus on the good sides and the future friendships.

People around the world are good. It doesn't matter what the news says because often the news is just that, news. The bad news is better than good news for the TV, but it's not real life. People are good. There is no difference between us, where you come from, what your religion is or what type of skin color you have. We're all the same, and we all desire the same things. Shelter, love, and food for us and our families. It's always been like that, and it will never change. Be friendly and treat the people the way you want to be treated and remember the best weapon you can use is your smile.

******

Top 10 Things You need to take on a Motorcycle Trip

After my last trip to Mongolia, I received many questions about my luggage. What I took with me, how I packed, how heavy it was etc. Many of you guys think that on the long trip, you need a lot of stuff, but it's not really like that at all.

I'm going to tell you the most important things that you should have in your motorcycle luggage. I would repeat it once again, the most important things, which means that if I don't have it, you have to stop, you have to find it, take it from the friend or buy it.

These are things that you would really need and use all the time. You can take whatever you like. You can double or triple all of your clothes, you can take computer, tablet, or smart phone at the same time, and you can also carry 50 different charges or cables because you might need them. You can pack a suit and tie for evenings in the restaurant. You can even take your mother in law if you like. Whatever you take, it will be loaded on your motorcycle, so my opinion doesn't really matter, but keep in mind that the most important things and the things you might need are two different things.

Soft luggage or hard cases - it is your personal choice. As you already know, I travel with soft luggage, and actually, in one 50 litters bag I carry everything I need. It's only 19 kilograms, but it was more than enough for a long motorcycle trip. Actually, I can easily spare maybe two or three kilograms more. Inside of the bag I carry everything I need. It's only 19 kilograms, but it was more than enough for the 35-day trip. Actually, I can easily spare maybe two or three kilograms more. Inside I keep all the luggage in small waterproof bags. There are two reasons to do this. The first one is obvious, to keep everything dry because nothing is 100 percent waterproof. The second is because sometimes when we sleep in hotels or guest houses, we'll park the motorcycles in the hotel's backyard or in the garage, so they are safe, and I do not take all of my stuff. I just take what I need. I can take my clothes, my toothbrush, cables, whatever I need, anything else stays on the bike.

Now, I will tell you exactly what I take.

Number 1

Rain gear. The reason I start with this is that I really believe that this is one of the most important things you should have with you. Some of you guys, including my riding friend Dima, will disagree with me, and the biggest argument will be that if you have a good quality waterproof riding gear, you don't really need rain gear. I have Rev it, and Dima has Rukka, so these are some of the top brands at the moment. On our last trip to Mongolia, Dima did not take his rain gear, which is meant that in case he got wet, we had to stop. Even though I had mine, we have to stop because of him. Both Dima's Rukka and my Rev it, are both waterproof, but nothing lasts forever. After about four or five hours, it starts to leak around your neck, under the helmet, around your gloves or through the gloves, even if your jacket and pants keep you dry, you'll start to feel the dampness and the cold after that. It is the same story with your boots and your gloves, so sooner or later your gear, your jacket, and your pants will be soaked with water. Yes, inside you will be dry, but the gear will not be, which means that you have to ride it to dry it and give the wind enough time to dry it. If not, you will need heating, but what about if it has rained for a whole week or a whole month? If your hotel room is very small, without any heating or even worse, you have to camp somewhere. If you cannot dry your gear, the water will penetrate the membrane gore-tex or whatever membrane you have, and we'll go inside, which means that on the next day you will have to ride completely wet. How long can you ride for wet? Don't make this mistake.

Always take your rain gear with you even if the forecast predicts nice weather.

Number 2

Clothes. I have four t-shirts, three with short sleeves and one which is long sleeved. I use the same to ride the bike and to walk around the cities. One switcher in case it is colder which I can use underneath my jacket as well. Zipped pants with removable leggings, very light, both the pants and t-shirt are from synthetic materials, so in case I need to wash them, they will be dry in just a couple of hours. Walking shoes and flip-flops. I have four pairs of socks, two for riding which are a bit longer and

two short pairs of socks for walking around. Underwear, three pieces. I don't have thermal underwear, don't need it on long trips, and I always have my riding gear with warm linings.

Number 3

Tools and spare parts. I don't have to explain to you just how important they are. Usually, I keep everything I will need in a plastic box.

Number 4

Camping gear. To carry camping gear or not really depends on your personal preferences and the type of the trip you are going to make. For example, on our trip to Mongolia, we used the tents only once. I carry all my camping gear: tent, mattress, sleeping bag, foldable chair, pillow, etc. in a bag. It weighs about four kilograms. It's a bit heavy, but in case I cannot find a hotel, or I want to save money, or I find a nice and beautiful spot to camp I can do it on the side with that. I also have my cooking stuff, my stove and everything else. **Do I have to take it all with me?**

So, for example, if you plan to spend the night in a paid camping area, there will probably be stoves, cooking stuff and everything you need. The only moment when you're going to need it is if you camp somewhere in the wild.

Number 5

Medical kit. This is something very important, and you have to make the selection carefully. Do not take the first one from the shop, customize it exactly for all of your needs. Inside you have to have everything that you might need on the trip, including pills for diarrhea or something like that.

Number 6

GPS and maps. As we all know, navigation is a very important part of your trip. My advice is to have both GPS and paper maps. The paper map, I always keep in my saddle bag. Usually, the GPS stays in front of me on the dashboard, but if I don't need it, I keep both in my tank bag.

Number 7

Charges and cables. Actually, I don't have that many. I have two cables, two sockets, and only a few more items. I carry everything in a small bag and as you know, most of the modern devices, like, computers, tablets, smart phones or even cameras are rechargeable with a simple USB plug. I keep that small bag in my tank bag.

Number 8

Spare keys. Do not forget to take the spare key of your motorcycle and all the locking mechanisms you have with you. If you travel alone, keep it in your riding gear, not on your motorcycle. If possible, make a secret pocket. If you have a riding friend, just exchange your keys.

Number 9

Disc lock and other locks. I don't think I have to tell you how important it is to protect your motorcycle.

Number 10

Spare visor or goggles.

So, guys, this is pretty much everything I carry with me. I did not mention some small things like a toothbrush or some additional gadgets because they weigh nothing and do not require any additional space. As you know, I travel very light, but it doesn't mean that you have to be the same.

******

How to choose the right riding gear for a long trip

There are plenty of motorcycle gear companies and brands on the market today. Actually, when you go to one of the biggest shops, you are faced with thousands of models, colors, materials and more. You are primarily there to choose the gear, but you get totally confused. It is much easier when you have a planned budget to spend and you are limited to just a few models.

On the other hand, when you really like to choose the right model, you have to be very well informed or you have to ask in the shop. Most of the guys there will help you with pleasure, but some of them have never rode a bike. So how they can help you, if they do not know? I am not telling you that everybody in these shops is a doom, but there are thousands of models, do you think that they test them all? Or, do you still believe in the labels the manufacturer wrote?

So, what should you buy? Summer or winter clothes? With or without inner lining? Textile, mesh or leather jacket?

Too many questions!

Here you have another one:

What you going to do if you have to cross many countries and the weather is changing every 500kms?

You can't take everything you need. Even if you have the biggest Honda Goldwin, the space will be limited.

I have made a lot of experiments. I tried to ride the whole season with a winter jacket and it was too hot in the summer. The summer jacket was too cold in the winter. On some trips, I even wore one jacket and kept the second in the luggage, but it was too heavy and one of the jackets I never used.

How to choose? Well, I do not have a universal answer, but I can tell you what I know:

1. When I buy clothes, I want to feel good with the style. It needs to be comfortable. I have to be able to move freely and to have possibility to wear another layer of extra clothes under it. It

doesn't matter what the guy from the shop will say, I am the one wearing the clothes, not him! The gear needs to have a warm, removable lining. Do not forget, sometimes you have to stay with this gear more than 10-12 hours per day. It is not unusual to sleep in it. You have to feel like it is a second skin.

2. The material has to be waterproof. There is no such a thing as 100% waterproof. All clothes at some stage start to leak. It is a matter of time, when you will be wet. In 5 minutes, 15 minutes or after few hours. Believe me, there is a big difference here. If you want to keep yourself dry, you have to buy rain weather gear.

3. I always buy the gear with integrated waterproof lining. There are some removable options, which you can add before it starts to rain. That's ok, but sometimes is not possible. For example: You are riding on the highway and it is starting to rain. You have no chance to stop and until you get to the sideway, so will be completely wet. Also, when you do not wear it, you have to find a place to store it and it needs to be easily assessable. When the lining is integrated all of that is not necessary. There are two types of integrated linings, visible – you can touch it and see it and covered with thin mesh cover on the top. If possible, always buy a second and I will explain why:

    When the weather is hot, you are sweating a lot, because of the waterproof lining. It is made from breathing material, but it is still holding the heat. When you become wet, the visible lining (without mesh cover) gets stuck to the skin. The worst part is on the pants. They actually get stuck to your legs as a clue. It is very weird sensation and it is definitely not good. Also, every time, when you need to jump on your bike, you have to lift your legs. Because of the already stuck lining, this is very difficult. It is the same as you wearing tight jeans. It is happened a few times with me, but once, while trying to sit on the bike, I broke the lining. A big hole was opened right in front of my balls. I said "Nothing to worry about, it is inside" but half an hour later, it starts to rain and all the water was going guess where? So, when I come back home, the pants went straight into the garbage. All of that could have been avoided if I had covered lining. It doesn't stick to your skin.

4. Clothes need to have a ventilation pockets, As a minimum 4 on the jacket and two on the pants. You will be so pleased when the temperatures goes over 30C.

5. Choose the models with as many possible pockets. You will fill them all. If possible, choose the model with the bigger pockets on the bag as well. Very useful.

6. Buy clothes with buttons and Velcro, never only with Velcro. It will get old, and after few months, it will not stick anymore. When you have buttons, you can still close your pockets.

7. Gloves: The same as the clothes, there are not 100% waterproof. Buy a minimum of two types. One very light (mesh) for the hot days and one waterproof. I carry simple medical gloves with me and wear them when it is raining or when it becomes really cold.

8. Boots: There is enough information about the boots and mixable opinions about what should you take. Once again, there are no universal boots. To have the maximum protection, to be waterproof and as comfortable as running shoes.

    I am sorry, but right at this moment, these type of boots have not yet been designed. It is all a matter of compromises. It is a personal choice which is best for you. There is no one-size-fits-all approach. The one with more protection, or the one with the nice design. If they are waterproofed, ok. If not, you can buy a rain cover, and you will be fine. Whatever you choose, please make sure that they are made from real leather, and they are breathable. Do not always believe the manufacturers. Test the boots before you go. Make a ride on a hot day.

Minimum 5-6 hours on the temperatures over 30C. When you get home, take it off and smell it. If there is even a simple indication of dampness, buy a new model.

I will tell you a funny story: I bought myself some nice shoes. Leather, breathable, or at least this was written on the label. I rode with those boots few times. They seemed nice and comfortable. I spent more than 4,000km riding in them with no problem at all, but it was not hot. Later on, during that same trip, we were in Azerbaijan. Riding all day and the temperatures were over 40C. We spent more than 15 hours in that heat. I had a feeling that my feet were boiling. I thought that is just too hot. Later in the evening, we were in a small ferry cabin that was the size of a prison cell. I took the boots off and wayyyyyyyyy... My feet were so damp like they had been soaked in the bath for hours. I can't explain to you what smell came out...it was like ammonia. It was impossible to ride with these boots for any longer. I took out a knife and cut the lining.

What a surprise! The manufacturer said that they are waterproof, yes, they are, but the waterproof lining was just a piece of nylon. They are waterproof, but not breathable whatsoever.

******

Motorcycle Camping Gear - what do you really need?

Camping gear is a very important part of every motorcycle adventure. It will give you some independence. You won't need to worry about hotels, reservations, bookings and so on, but I have one important question for you:

Do you really need it?

Before any long-distance trip, please do some research and find some information for the area you are going to travel in, the weather forecasts, what is the average temperature for the season you are going to travel in, what is the elevation, is it hot, is it cold, is it raining, is it dry and so on

When you have that information, you can find out that you do not actually need your camping gear.

For example, when I was in Central Asia for about 2 months I used my gear only 3 times. So is it worth it to have it on my bike all the time for 17,000 kilometers, to load it and unload it every day and use it just 3 times? Is it worth it? I do not know, you tell me. From these 3 times, only 1 was necessary. The other 2 were just personal choice. We had an option to sleep somewhere, but we decided to camp. The 3rd one was necessary because we were in the middle of the Karakum Desert, so we had no choice, we had to camp.

Another example is my journey to Norway. Norway is an expensive country as most of the Scandinavian countries. The hotels are very expensive, the food is very expensive, everything is around double the price you would usually pay so I brought my camping gear and camped every single day. Because of the prices, because my budget at that time was tight and so on, I had to camp.

So, in the first case in Asia, I didn't really need it, but in the second case, it was absolutely necessary. I said you do not need it in Asia now, I am going to give you some information about why. Most of the guest houses in that area are very cheap, many costing just $10 per night. Here, you can have bed, bath, dinner, and breakfast. So for $10, it is not just not worth sleeping in a tent.

Another reason not to camp is that the temperatures are over 40 degrees. When you are outside and the temperature is over 40 degrees, trust me when I say that the last thing you will want after a whole day of traveling is to be camping.

Another example is from my trip to Morocco for 30 days, and I never used my tent once during this trip. So I have this big bag, weighing about 7 kilograms on top of my bike, I had it for 1 month more than 14,000 kilometers but never used it.

In my last trip to Mongolia I use it only once.

Another topic to think twice is the weight of your camping gear. In the best case, it is going to be around 5-10 kilograms. I know some of you guys will say: "Oh 10 kilograms that's nothing, I need my camping gear I want to be independent" It is not exactly like that. Any weight matters at some stage, especially if you have to ride a lot of off-road or maybe you have to ride on sand, then you will definitely fall at some point. Every time you fall, you have to lift your bike. If you have a heavy bike with a lot of top luggage, it will be a problem.

So, what I am trying to say is that if you are going to use your camping gear just for a day or two, for a trip that is a month or two long, just leave it at home. You can thank me later.

Let's talk about the camping gear now.

1. Tent

The tent is the most important part of your camping gear, it is actually your mobile home. This is the place where you are going to rest when you finish your riding day. Make sure you choose the right tent with enough space for you to be comfortable inside. If you are one person take a tent for a minimum of 2 people. That way, you will have more space for you and for your luggage in case you need it. The brand and the shape do not matter but your tent needs to be waterproof, and one very important thing is to learn how to open and close it before you go. Do some experiments and get some experience, trust me, it will help you in the long run. You will not have to worry about figuring out how to erect your tent after a long day of riding which again, you will thank me for this advice later.

2. Mattress

I used a simple foam mattress. It is very light and doesn't take up much space, but, I will admit that it was not comfortable. So I changed it to an air mattress. It is very comfortable, around 3 or 4 centimeters in depth and provides the comfort I need. So once again, it is very important after a long day of riding to have a nice place to rest. If your mattress is not very comfortable on the next day you will be exhausted. It is very important to choose the right model to suit your sleeping style and your body.

3. Sleeping bag

Choose your sleeping bag carefully. About 3 years ago, I was sleeping in my tent in the Alps, and I had a very light sleeping bag. For the whole night, I was freezing to death. I needed to put on all of my clothes and all of my riding gear, hat, gloves and even the riding boots to survive. When that terrible night finished I promised myself, in future I will have a nice warm sleeping bag. I also have a very small air pillow. It requires minimal space when the air is out, and it weighs next to nothing, but it is very comfortable and I would not be without it.

4. Foldable chair

I found one that is very small and light. It looks very unserious, but actually it is very strong. I am 100 kilograms and have used this many times, it is still going strong and is showing no signs of serious wear yet.

5. Cooking Stuff

I have a small cup, and inside I keep everything I am going to need such as sugar, a lighter, some tea, salt, spoon, fork and a knife. It is very light, and it requires only minimal space. I use a petrol cooking stove. It is very light and very simple. The reason I chose the stove with petrol is that I always have petrol. I have 2 towels. One small, to dry my face or hands and the second is big, it is about my size if I need to take a shower, both of them are made of microfiber they are very light and require very little space. They are also really quick-drying as well which helps with time and weight.

The most important requirements for your camping gear are that they are light and take up as little space as possible. I also carry some fast food like spaghetti or rice, so everything I need is easily achieved with just a little boiling water, and in about 10 minutes I am ready to eat. I also carry a small metal cup which I use for water, tea and even vodka sometimes too – only after riding for the day is complete! Another very important part of your gear is a mosquito mesh if you are going to sleep in an area with a lot of mosquitoes. If you choose the right motorcycle gear, it will all fit into one medium waterproof bag.

******

What tires do I need for my motorcycle trip?

To buy the right tires for a long motorcycle trip sounds like a really difficult task. There are so many different opinions about it: street, dual-sport or knobby. Here I will tell you about the most popular options and give you some very practical advice on how to choose the right tires.

So many different experts and sellers will try to convince you that their tires are much better than others or that they will have better traction and last longer.

First of all, and very important is to understand that there are no universal tires. Every choice is a compromise. For example, 100% street tire will work great on the asphalt, but very poor on off-road and absolutely useless in the mud. On the other hand, knobby tires will be perfect on a motocross track, but terrible on the street. Because of that, during the years, the big companies started to produce different variations: sport, touring, adventure, dual-sport or any kind of creative names to make us believe that their tires are the best.

But what is best for one could be the worst for another. It is very subjective and depends on many different factors:

- The weight of your bike
- The type of roads you are going to ride
- Your riding style
- The mileage you plan to cover during your trip
- The temperatures in your time schedule

Each one of these factors could help your tire to last longer or destroy it faster. Let's have a look at some of the most popular options:

Number 1. Road tires or touring tires

They will be probably 90% road and 10% off-road orientated. Examples are Continental Road Attack or Michelin Pilot. The reason of that is because they will have a much larger surface area in contact with the road. The block will be much wider, and the channels will not be that deep. Because of that, the bike will be more stable when you ride it at high speed or when cornering for example. Because of the large surface area, they provide a much longer mileage. These tires are perfect for long trips where you will stay on the asphalt for 90% of the time. Ok, what will the other 10% will give you? Nothing, it is just a good marketing strategy to sell the model easier and reach that small percent of possible buyers who might want to try some off-road terrains.

Number 2. Adventure Tires

They will be 80% - 20%, 70%-30% or even 60%-40% road vs. off-road orientated. Some examples are the Mitas 07and Heidenau K60 scout. Here we can see hugely different structures. The blocks are not that big, and they have wider channels between. Also, they have this large central line, which helps them to have a longer mileage compared to some of the competitors. These tires will provide good traction on the pavement, but also decent grip when you ride off-road as well. That basically means that you can ride on the road, but also in some light off-road sections, such as gravel, smooth dirt roads, some rocky terrains, but no mud or hard off-road terrain. You can, but it really depends on your riding skills and the weight of your motorcycle. These are a very good option for those who plan a long trip, but with possible off-road sections.

Number 3. Dual-sport or more aggressive tires.

They are usually 50%-50% or even 40%-60% road vs. off-road orientated. The good examples are Continental TKC 80 or Metzeler Karroo 3. Here we can see that the blocks are smaller and the channels are wider, and the center line does not exist. Also, the sharp edges here will dig into the soft ground and will hold your bike much better. The larger gaps, between the blocks, will allow the tire to self-clean from the mud while you ride. Of course, all of this comes at a certain price point. On the road, these tires will be more flexible and a little tricky on the corners, especially when you have worn them out a little. Another downside is that they finish pretty quickly. I really like the TKC 80 and use them in almost all of my trips, because they give me the confidence I need both on and off-road. However, I have to confess that the mileage they provide is not very much. You have to keep in mind that if you ride a heavy dual sports bike, like the GS 1200 or the Super Tenere and you ride mostly on the highways, they will finish even quicker. These tires are the perfect solution if you plan a trip with a lot of off-road mileage and you want to have the best possible traction.

Remember these very simple rules:

-The purpose of any tire is to provide the best possible traction. If the tire finishes quickly that means that it is made from more rubber and less plastic.

-The life of any tire depends on its shape, structure, the motorcycle, the roads and the riding style of the rider.

As I said in the beginning, there are no universal tires. As usual, I will try to give you the best possible advice, but now instead of answers, I will ask you some quick questions:

- Which material provides more traction, rubber or plastic?
- What is more important, your life or the life of the tires?
- What type of bike do you have?
- How many km do you plan to ride on your trip?
- How fast do you ride normally?
- Are you planning to cover any off-road terrain on your trip? If yes, how many km?

When you answer these questions, you will know what type of tires you need to get for your long-distance motorcycle trip.

******

What to take and how to pack for your long-distance motorcycle trip?

As I have already told you many times, weight matters. The last thing you would want to have on a long motorcycle trip is a heavy bike. Mostly weighed down with stuff you will never or rarely use. Every person is different, and everybody has different priorities. I am not going to try to change you, but I will tell you what I do and what I have learned over the years.

First and foremost, when I pack, I always make a very simple list. Camping gear, Tent, mattress, sleeping bag, pillow, foldable chair, some stuff like toothpaste, gel, some tea, metal cup, cooking stove, bottle for petrol, 2 towels, cooking stuff and some food.

Clothes

Pants that are very light, 2 riding t-shirts, another one with long sleeves, and a switcher. All of these clothes are made from synthetic material so that when I wash them, after only 30 minutes, they are dry. Spare gloves, flip flops, walking shoes, 3 pair of socks that are synthetic and 3 underwears.

Tools and spare parts

I carry only basic things like zip ties, spark plugs, voltage regulator, some cables, chain locks, spare clutch and duck-tape that's everything. In a small bag, I keep all tools which I need to fix a flat tire. I have another set of tools, for everything I use on my bike.

Electronics

also have all the cables and chargers I will need on the road. A small camera, a helmet camera is the one I use to record from my helmet and tablet which I use instead of a computer because it is lighter, and you can keep it in your riding jacket with ease.

Medical kit

It is very important for the kit to be customized exactly for you. If you need some pills of any kind, then make sure you have them on the road.

That is basically everything. When you follow the list, it is almost impossible to forget the important things. Believe me, the items on this list are more than enough. What you need and what you must have are 2 different things. Even if you load your bike with 50 extra kilograms, you will always miss something, and you will always need more.

So, my advice is to you is to pack as light as possible and you will be amazed how much easier the ride will go as a result of this.

******

Top ten tips for riding your motorcycle over a long distance.

The most commonly asked question is:

"How many kilometers per day am I going to be riding?"

Well, there is no answer to that question. It is very subjective, and it depends on many circumstances. For example, when I am riding, on the highway I can go between 1000-1200 kilometers, on the normal roads I can go between 500-800 kilometers, and on roads with bad conditions or off-road I can't go more than 200-300 kilometers per day.

So maybe the right question is:

"How many hours per day?"

But again it is the same story. If there is nice weather, if I feel good, and if we have daylight I can ride up to 15-16 hours. If the weather is bad, if it is raining, if it is in the winter and the day is short I can ride 8 hours or 4 hours, I do not know. There is no mathematical equation or some kind of logic about how long you can ride for or how many kilometers you can cover per day. I can't give you an answer about how long you can ride for, but what I can give you are 10 tips for riding long distances on your bike.

Tip Number 1: Start

Always wake up before sunrise. If you do, you will have enough time for your breakfast, to prepare your bike, maybe even to check some news and so on.

Tip Number 2: Luggage

Pack your bag and tie it securely on your motorcycle. Make sure that all you are going to need on the road are in a place where you can easily access when you need them.

Tip Number 3: Petrol

Always refill your bike before you go to sleep. On the next day it will be ready and waiting for you.

Tip Number 4: Timing

Ride very strict. Never ride for more than 2 hours and never stop for more than 30 minutes. In both cases, you lose your concentration. Use these breaks to refill your tank at the same time, if you do it this way you save precious time. Riding with a high speed will not help you to recover lost time, and you might get involved in an accident or even die, it's just not worth the risk.

Tip Number 5: Food

Always have a nice breakfast before you go. It will give you enough energy to ride until lunch time without even thinking about food. When you get hungry after breakfast, please eat as light as possible. Things like beef steaks or McDonald's are not recommended. Keep some chocolate bars or nuts in your pockets in case you need them on the road. You don't want to get too tired, too early on in the day and eating large meals can easily make you feel like you need a sleep.

Tip Number 6: Water

Drink a lot of water. Use a Camel Bag instead of a normal bottle of water because when you have a Camel Bag system, you can drink at any time, even while you are riding. Usually what happens is that when you are riding in poor conditions, you do not have the time, or you do not want to stop to drink your water, but when you have a Camel Bag, you can drink all the time without needing to stop. Keep in mind that when riding, your body consumes double the water so do not allow yourself to get dehydrated as it will be a big problem. You will start to lose concentration and begin to feel sick.

Tip Number 7: Backpack

Keep it as light as possible. Even 2 kilograms will be a big problem after a couple of hours. You will start to feel pressure around your shoulders and in the end your backpack will end up tied onto your bike or in the garbage. I recommend you use a body vest instead of a backpack. When you have a body vest, it is all the way around your body and you can ride with it all day without any problems. Something to do with weight distribution, I don't know, but I do know it works.

Tip Number 8: Coffee

Coffee is a very powerful stimulant. Some people can't live without coffee. My advice is to stop drinking coffee, but if you can't, just make sure you bring enough for when you are on the road. In some places like Asia for example, it is very difficult to find coffee, especially when you are on the oad. So, if you can't deal with your coffee addiction, make sure you have enough for each day of your trip. The coffee addiction is real, and you do not need to test it when you are on the road, believe me.

Tip Number 9: Communication

If you ride in a group, make sure that all of you have a nice Bluetooth system. Sena is a nice brand, and you can connect up to 8 devices. When you have communication between your riding partners, it is a completely different story. If you ride alone, bring some earplugs. They make a huge difference. In the past, when I was riding between 12-14 hours a day without earplugs, later in the evening, when I would go to bed and try to sleep, I struggled because my head was buzzing all the time. I needed an hour or sometimes even two hours so that I could get relaxed and sleep. When you are wearing earplugs, all of this can be avoided.

Tip Number 10: Stop on time

Always stop on time. The best time to stop is before sunset. You need to have enough time to find your hotel, to have dinner, to unload your bike, to prepare yourself for the next day, to check the maps and maybe see something from the area you are staying in. It is very important to do it this way so the next morning you wake up fresh and ready to go.

One bonus piece of advice for you is that a long motorcycle trip is not a race. Please do not ride fast. There is nobody that counts your time. It doesn't matter how fast you are going. It doesn't matter at that moment; or at the next bend how fast you will go through the corner and how fast you will get out of the corner. Once again, it is not a race, 30 seconds more, 1 minute more or 1 hour more, it doesn't matter the most important part of your journey is to get to the point you planned and of course, to come back home safe and in one piece.

******

Top 10 Accessories you should have on a Long Motorcycle Trip

If you are still wondering, what to take with you and what are the necessary items that you are going to need for a motorcycle trip, it is time to find out.

Number 1

Tank bag. Many riders do not have one, but for me, this is the most useful bag you can have on a motorcycle trip. Inside, I keep only important things like my GPS, camera, maps, smart phone and stuff like that. Some of my riding friends say they do not need it because they have a top case. Yes, maybe the top case is a very good solution for city riding because you can even keep your helmet inside but on the long trips, especially if you plan to have some rough terrain or off-road, the top case could cause you many problems. From unexpected shaking, up to a bent or even broken subframe. Another good reason for me to choose a tank bag instead of a top case is that I can take it with me. It can hold all of my necessary things and I can take it with me when I walk around the cities.

Number 2

Heated grips. I am sure that this is something which everybody will agree upon. Once you have them, it will be very difficult to travel without them. Yes, if you live in an area with a warm climate it is a different story, but if you have plans to travel the world, they will be necessary.

Number 3

12 V mini USB socket. This small item costs nothing compared to the rest of the accessories but it is very important to keep all of your electronic devices working. There are thousands of models on the market, the brand or the shape doesn't really matter. However, I will recommend that you have at least 2 because it is very easy to forget it or lose it somewhere.

Number 4

Bluetooth. Having this device is such a pleasure. I never really connect my smartphone or listen to the radio, but having communications with your riding companions is just crazy. When you have your Bluetooth, it is like a whole new world, the only problem is that you get addicted, and it will be very difficult to travel without it after that.

Number 5

Voltmeter. I highly recommend having one of these devices. It will give you the chance to constantly monitor the condition of your alternator and your battery. In the instance of any possible fails you will find out on time, and you can stop and fix them quickly.

Number 6:

Thermometer. "Oh come on, thermometers are everywhere" Really? How many degrees is it now, without looking around you? Tell me how many degrees it is? "Why is it so important to know," who cares about that." I will try to explain. When you travel with a motorcycle the weather is very important. When you have a thermometer on your bike, you will know how exactly you feel at a certain temperature. This means that next time, you will know exactly what kind of clothes you need. For example, if it is less than 18 degrees you need to put your warm linings on, and above 25 degrees, you do not need them and also may have to remove your long sleeves or something like that. It sounds obvious, but believe me it is not like that. I have seen so many people with too many clothes or too fewer clothes than needed. Two degrees up or down could make a significant difference in your riding comfort. Of course, if you have a new model of bike, then probably you are going to have a thermometer on the dashboard, and you won't need to worry about it.

Number 7

Pin lock. This is basically an anti-fog lens that is attached inside of your visor, if your helmet has it, great. If you do not have it, you can buy universal and mount it. Riding with a fogged visor could be really annoying not to mention being quite dangerous. You will understand this point more, on the first time when you have to ride in the cold days or in the rain.

Number 8

Camel Bag. When you ride a motorcycle, your body consumes double or triple the amount of water compared to its normal processes. It is very important to drink enough, especially if you ride in the hot weather. Some of you will disagree and say that a simple bottle of water is the same, but it is not the same. When you have a Camel Bag, you can drink water even while you ride and this is very important. It is comfortable to wear and doesn't interfere too much with your riding gear. Sometimes, you have to ride for many hours without stopping. For example, on the highway, in bad weather or off-road and you can disagree and say "Yea, that is true, but I can stop after 2 hours maybe". To drink once every 2 hours will not be enough if it is a hot day. It is very easy to dehydrate yourself, and once you get dehydrated, you will start to lose concentration, and as you know, this can be very dangerous.

Number 9

Air Pump. As you know, sometimes shit just happens. A compressor or a simple pump can save your adventure in many situations. Take one of these and always keep it with you, you do not need to learn it the hard way like I did.

Number 10

Visor Cleaner. When you are on a long trip, especially in the Summer, you will catch a lot of flies and mosquitoes with your visor. In theory, you do not really need it because you can clean your visor with anything, even with water. That is correct, but I skip it on many occasions because I have no water. I even tried to use the water from my Camel bag sometimes too. I sucked from the Camel Bag and spat it on to the visor to try to and clean it. This was stupid, and I couldn't actually clean it properly this way. This visor cleaner liquid contains alcohol which removes the bugs from your visor very easily. They are also really small so you can carry them with ease.

******

Money for Motorcycle Trips - Cash or Credit cards?

When we travel, we need money. That is obvious, but in what currency? Should we carry cash or should we use a credit or debit card? Where do we hide it, how do we change it, and many more questions of this nature come to mind.

When you plan your first trip, you have so many things to worry about that you almost forget about the money. I am not talking about the actual cost of the trip, I am sure you have already found enough information about how much exactly is it going to cost you? I am talking about the money itself. It is obvious you are going to need it, but in what currency, credit or debit cards? Unfortunately, I do not have one universal answer, but I will give you 3 very useful tips that work in 99% of the countries around the world.

Number 1

Split the money. Let me explain what I mean here. Everybody knows about cash, and when you have it, all doors are open. Yes, they are, but to carry a lot of money in cash is not always the best solution. You can lose it, forget it somewhere, be robbed or in the worst scenario, if you have an accident and you need to be transported to the hospital for surgery, it could easily get mislaid. In all of those cases, you do not have any actual control of your cash. That's why I always split the money - 50% cash, 50% credit cards. Let me give you more details. Every time I have the opportunity to pay with my credit card, debit card or whatever you have, I take it. The cash I have, I will always keep for the moments when that is not going to be possible.

In Europe, all petrol stations and almost every hotel or restaurant will accept your credit card. Actually, these are most of the main costs when you travel. If you can pay for all of those services with your credit card, you do not need to carry so much cash. The cash you are going to keep for places like South America, Asia or Africa and even there in the big cities, you can pay with a credit card. As I said earlier, you have to split your money - credit card and cash but also it is a very good idea to split your cash into 2 or 3 different places. For example, you can have a small amount in your pocket just for your daily expenses. You can keep some notes in your wallet in case, never put it all there in case somebody decides to take your wallet, and the rest of the money, just hide , it somewhere. I am not going to tell you where I hide my money, because it is a secret; but I am sure you can find more than enough places in your luggage, clothes or wherever you decide to stash it.

Number 2

Currency. What currency you should keep your money in? Well, it really depends on the type of trip you are going to have and the destination you are going to. It is obvious that if you plan to travel to Europe, it is going to be the Euro, but outside of Europe, I will recommend you keep only dollars. Why dollars? The Euro is an international currency, and everybody knows about it? Not really, in many places around the world they have never seen Euros. Yes, in the banks they know what it is and can change it, but sometimes you have to change with locals or in your hotel or restaurant, and if the person there has never seen it before, it will not be possible. With dollars, it is much easier. In most of the cases, the conversion rate of the dollar will be much higher than the conversion rate of the Euro.

Another good tip is to keep small notes like 5, 10 or even 20 dollars because sometimes you have to pay for your guest house and it costs $10, but the owner of the house will not have $90 in change. He might have it, but not always. It is the same story when you have to change money. I will give you a funny example. We were in Uzbekistan, and the conversion rate was 3,300 UZB for 1 dollar, so actually, when you exchange $100, you receive one big plastic bag with money. Fair enough, you can spend it easily because the numbers mean nothing there. Actually, you are going to drink tea or beer with 5000 or even 10000 of their currency. But, it is still a big plastic bag of money, and you have to keep it somewhere. For example, when you travel with a motorcycle, you know space is limited. If you can change only 10, 20 or 50 dollars, it is much better that way.

Number 3

Credit cards. Which system is better; Visa, MasterCard or American Express? The best answer is all of them. Outside of the states, American Express is not really useful. In Europe, for example, they will accept it in many restaurants or hotels, but you will be charged additional 7% payment fee for the pleasure of using that card. The company which provides these post terminal machines or the machines which are used to charge your card will usually charge about 2-3% for Visa and MasterCard, and 7% for American Express. This means that if you have a hotel and somebody pays you will American Express, you will receive in your bank account 7% less money, that's why they will charge you an additional 7-10%, just to cover their costs. Believe me, I had a business in Germany for many years and I know what I am talking about. Okay, then the solution will be to use American Express for any payments in the States and Visa when you go to Europe or around other parts of the world.

That is okay, but when I was in Russia in 2015, Visa had some problems with the Russian government and 90% of the payments were being refused, they weren't actually working. I think it was part of the sanctions against Russia because of the invasions in Ukraine, I am not sure about the details, but on the other hand, MasterCard was fine and working well.

Another topic to consider is the bank's permissions and commissions when you use your credit card abroad. You have to inform the credit card company where you're going, and usually, you have to check your withdrawal limits. I have had many American clients that came to Berlin, and after they arrived, then realized they cannot draw any money from the cash machines. This is not a big deal, you can call your bank and explain the situation to them, and everything will be fine, but if you are in Europe you have 7, 8, 9 or 11 hours difference which means you will have to wait for the proper hours when your bank will open before it is possible for somebody to pick up the telephone and release your cards. If you are in the petrol station with a full tank and no money, what are you going to do? Wait there for 8 hours? That's why it is always better to check in advance.

Also, keep in mind that from 2017, most of the banks changed their rules. I am not sure about your own bank, but it is worth checking this out and knowing the information in advance of your trip. Because if, for example, the withdrawal limits on the cash machines now in Europe are 1500 Euro per day or 2500 Euro per week. Of course, this sounds like more than enough money for your travels, but what if you have a problem with your bike - a breakdown where you will have to change expensive parts or even the whole engine. If you have, for example, 2000 Euros for a new engine, you will be left with only 500 Euros for the whole week. That's why I always say that preparation is the key to success. Make and check everything when you are at home, well in advance of your departure date.

******

The best navigation for a Long Motorcycle trip - GPS or Paper Map?

So guys, GPS or paper; what should you take on a long motorcycle trip? That is a really nice question, and I have a very simple answer, but before I tell you what I think; let's discuss the pros and cons of the competitors.

I'll start with GPS. It is an absolutely great device. It has so much information that I cannot even imagine traveling without it.

Number 1

More information. Even on a very cheap and simple device, there is so much information. You can play with them and use it all day long, and you will find everything you need: addresses, hotels, restaurants, attractions, garages, galleries, cash machines, and many more useful things. It is a device you absolutely must have especially when you're traveling around the cities.

Number 2

It is easy to use. Even a five-year-old kid or an eighty year old biker who refuses to use any technologies will be fine after just five minutes. You do not need to know anything about navigation, about the road planning, about the directions or about a compass. What you have to do is just choose the destination, press the button and follow the instructions, so simple. Once you have done it, it is almost impossible to return back to the old paper maps.

Number 3

You can use it while you are riding or even better you can connect it to your Bluetooth device, and just listen to the instructions. You do not need to pay any attention to it, which is of course even safer.

Number 4

It is easy and cheap to upgrade. You can download any map for half of the price of the same paper variant. The maps are much more the detailed and you can have many maps in just one simple device. You can switch between different maps with just one click, even while you are riding.

Number 5

Traffic information and calculations. All new models will update the traffic information and will find the best possible route for you to take. They will calculate everything and will show you all important numbers: kilometers and hours per day, average, constant, and top speeds, estimated riding hours or arrival time. All of this information could be priceless, especially if you're fighting with the time.

There are many more pros, but I think I have said enough on the matter now, these devices are absolutely brilliant. Now let's talk about the cons.

Number 1

Price, the new models like a "Garmin Zumo" for example, cost about $400 or more. I'm not saying that it is an impossible price for you guys, but because of that, I still use my old Garmin because I cannot find a really good or proper reason to spend $400 for a new GPS. If somebody wants to give me it as a gift, then of course I will take it and use it with pleasure.

Number 2

They need power to work the way I just explained. Because they need power, you have to prepare your motorcycle with a power outlet. If your bike does not have one, it sounds like a not so big problem, but let me give you one example. I was traveling in Madrid, Spain. Of course, the GPS was guiding me. Everything was fine until one very special moment when the device just blinked twice and then said "no power, the device will turn off in 20 seconds", because this is a very old device and because it always stayed plugged in the battery died many years ago, so when the power is off, it stops in just a few seconds. Yes, I will agree that with the new device, the battery will last much longer, but how much longer? 2-3 hours maximum. Anyway, I pulled over and stopped to investigate the problem, even though I already knew what the issue was, because the same thing happened a year earlier, with the same GPS. On my motorcycle, I have two power outlets, one on the left and one on the right. The left one stopped a year ago, so I started to plug my GPS into the right one. So, when it happened, I knew what the problem was. I stopped at the first possible safe location. It was not all that safe because it was raining and there were so many cars and people everywhere, but anyway, I didn't want to open my box to look for a sand paper or proper tools to clean out a power outlet. So, I just decided to clean it out with my pocket knife and guess what? It was fine until I touched the plus and minus and I burnt one of the fuses, and everything stopped. I am sure one of you guys will say: "Yeah, out on my power outlet I have a rubber core, so when I close it, the water cannot go inside." Yes, guys, I have the same, but to plug in your GPS, you need to open that core and then the water will be able to get in.

The story, of course, has a happy ending. Many years ago, I was living in Madrid and I was able to remember roughly where I was at that moment and with the help of the locals, I was able to find the address I needed. Of course, on the next day in the hotel when the weather was nice, I just cleaned it properly and fixed it and that's all, no major drama. This was just one example that the GPS systems are great devices when they work. You do tend to depend on them heavily when taking a long-distance trip on a motorcycle.

Number 3

With the GPS, you do not know exactly where you are at any moment. It sounds a little confusing, but let me explain it to you. When you use a GPS, it is the same as being a passenger in somebody else's car. You do not know what is in front of you, or what is on the left or right. You do not know what kind of town, villages or cities you have around you, and you do not know about rivers and bridges, in fact, you know nothing. You just watch this small screen, follow the instructions and that's all, and if the device stops exactly like the situation and I just explained, in most cases, you are totally lost.

Number 4

Possible theft. Every time you leave the bike, you have to take the GPS with you, unless you have some kind of a locking mechanism to protect it.

Number 5

Risk of draining your battery. It is a classic example to forget about the impact having a GPS plugged into your bike for a day, two or a week. It is not uncommon to find your battery flat as a result of this. Most of the power outlets are connected straight to the battery. When you turn off your key, it doesn't matter. It is still on, and the navigation will work until it drains your battery.

Now let's discuss paper maps. In this case, instead of pros, I will start with cons.

Number 1

You have to learn how to use them. It is not that difficult, but you have to spend some time to learn how to do it. If you used to be able to read maps then picking it up again shouldn't be too hard. To have an idea about the roads, directions, and symbols, you have to read the legend. Almost all maps use the same symbols, but if you have never read or if you have never seen one before, it is going to be tricky.

Number 2

Number of maps. If you're on a long trip with a lot of countries, you have to buy a map for each one of the countries, so at the end, you will need a bag or at least a big pocket to keep all of those maps stored in.

Number 3

You have to buy a tank bag. It is not necessary, but if you want to be able to use that map, you need a tank bag. A tank bag with a transparent pocket on the top, where you can put your map and where you will be able to read it. Of course, you can just keep it in your pocket, in your back or in your top case. It doesn't matter, but it does mean that each time when you need some directions, you need to stop, and you need to take out the map. If you have tank bag, you can just stop, look, and check.

Number 4

You cannot use it while you're riding. Actually, you can, but the letters are so small that you will need time to find it. This means that you will have to stop looking around you and focus on the map and of course, this will put you in serious danger. It is always better to stop and check it properly.

Number 5

Paper maps, do not last long. It depends on the quality of course, but usually, they last about one or two big trips. The problem is, because the maps are big and the bags are small. You have to fold it to the specific area you are at that moment and then fold it to the next one again and again. In the end, because all of that folding all the time, it will start to crack at the edges and finally, it will fall apart.

Let's talk about the pros. Actually, I found only two real pros of the paper maps against the GPS, but they are more than enough for me.

The first and most important is to find your bearings, to know exactly where you are going, and to be familiar with the whole location. Preparation is the key to success. With a paper map, you can see, and you will know everything. You will know ways of north, east, south or west, where the rivers fold, where the highways are, the main roads, the cities and more. Even if you lose it, you can just close your eyes, and you will remember so many details. The reason for that, is because during that trip guys, you're going to check the map so many times, that without even noticing, you'll remember most of the details and you will be able to remember the most important towns, roads, rivers, connections and duplicate it later.

I do not know for you guys, but I always prepare the route before I go. I sit at home with my map book open and a big marker and just draw the route I am going to take. I even put small dots for how many kilometers or what I have to expect. I just circle the most important points and many more.

I will give you one more example now guys. We were in Kazakhstan, and we were in the middle of nowhere when my friend burned his clutch. We were next to the road trying to fixing the clutch and solve the problem and so on. While we were doing this, my bike was sitting on the side of the road about 20 meters away from me and I was able to see it just fine, Then, a big truck stopped in front of it, so I was not able to see it for a short period of time. During that very short period of time, somebody tried to steal my GPS, of course they couldn't, but they did cut my cables. So, we finished with the bike, we loaded my friend's bike on the truck, he got into the truck, and they left. I had to meet them about 350 kilometers away in a small village next to the road. Of course, I turned on my motorcycle and the GPS and then I realized that the GPS wasn't working because the cable had been cut. So, it was dark and these cables are very thin, and my hands were covered in oil, so, I wasn't able to fix it at that moment. What I did, was I just tried to remember what I have seen on the map, because in Kazakhstan there are not actually so many roads, I actually remembered where I had to go because I had seen it so many times on the map and that's how I was able to get to the point I wanted to reach. Of course, later in the hotel when I was in a quiet atmosphere, I was able to fix the cables.

Second is the price. A good map will cost about $10-$15, maximum. Even if you have to buy five or six different maps, it will be much cheaper than a simple GPS device.

So guys, at the end I talked so much, and I did not answer the question. GPS or paper map?

I didn't answer because it is obvious. Use both the GPS and paper map. The GPS will guide you all the time, but the paper map is the one to help you when you really need it most. It's called having a back-up plan.

******

Top 5 Common Mistakes on a Long Motorcycle Trip - How to avoid them?

It doesn't really matter how good or how technical a rider you are, if you have never been on a long motorcycle trip before, you are bound to make at least one of these mistakes:

Number 1

Wrong motorcycle. It is very important to have the right bike. But what does that mean? How do you choose the one for you? I will try to explain it to you. Do not listen to what other people say, do not trust anyone about the type of motorcycle you should have on a long motorcycle trip. Only you will know how fast you are going to ride, how many kilometers per day you will ride and where you will go.

Only you are the person who can choose the right motorcycle.

What you need to do is to find all the information about the area you are going to travel in: terrains, roads, elevation, weather conditions and many more. Based on all of that information, you can then take the right decision and chose the proper bike. I have told you this many times I know, but I am going to tell you it again. Preparation is the key to success. I really respect the guys who travel without any plans or preparations, but for me this is nonsense. I prefer to be ready. I want to know where I am going and what I can expect there.

To go on a long motorcycle trip in Siberia, on the road of bones for example with a GS 1200 is not the right decision. The very last thing you are going to need on such trip is a heavy motorcycle. You have to choose the motorcycle for the hardest part of the trip, not for the easiest, which means that if you have a 10,000 km trip but 2,000 km are a hard off-road section, you have to prepare and choose the motorcycle for this 2,000 km. It will be much easier to ride a light motorcycle on the highway instead of a heavy beast off-road. On the other hand, to ride on Iron's buts competition, thousands of miles per day on the highway with something like a Suzuki DR 400 or a Honda 250 is going to be a really "enthusiastic" adventure. In both cases, if you have the wrong bike, it will be a terrible mistake.

I will tell you a funny story. Last year we were riding in the Alps. The temperature was about 5-6 degrees, so we were stopping more often than usual. During one of our breaks, next to us came a German rider with a Honda CBR and a leather suit. He parked next to us, but almost fell while doing so. After that, he just took his helmet and started shaking like a dancer, so I asked him if he is okay and he said: Yes, I am okay, but this fucking position and it is so cold. It was a clear example that this bike was not designed for that purpose. The sports bikes are great, but they are not designed for long motorcycle trips. Of course, you can complete a motorcycle trip with anything, even with a scooter, but if you have a proper bike, it is going to be so much easier and safer for you.

Number 2

Wrong gear choice. I have seen many riders make the same mistake. The German rider I just told you about is a perfect example; that the leather suit is great to go on the track or to ride in during the hot days, but is not made for a long motorcycle trip. It will work but not every day, and not in all conditions. Doing your research before the trip will help you during it. If the weather is going to be hot, you can take only a light jacket. If you have plans to cross the mountains, if it is Winter or if it is cold, then you have to choose a Winter jacket. Proper full-season, air ventilated gear is the best option. It will work in almost all conditions, it will never be perfect but it will work just fine. There is another group of riders-gear. I am sure you have seen them around. They will have everything they could possibly buy from highly expensive shops. They will have special hard cases, a bag designed to stay on the cases, a waterproof bag designed to stay on top, a unique GPS mount or any number of adventure gadgets. Their bike looks like a Christmas tree, and they won't use 90% of the stuff. If you are one of those guys, then I recommend you go on a simple 1-week trip and see what works and what doesn't work and next time take exactly what you need. Want to have and need to have are two very different things.

Number 3

Too much weight. Most of you guys already take too much stuff. To already have a heavy bike weighing 200-250 kg and to load it with an additional 50-60 kg on the top is not something I will ever do. Any weight will always matter, especially if you have plans to ride off-road. This heavy bike has only cons. There are many discussions about hard cases and soft luggage. If I say you take too much, I mean you do not actually need 10 t-shirts, 5 sets of jeans or trousers, 3 different types of shoes and shower gels. Guys, you are on a motorcycle trip not on a fashion week. Simple zip pants are more than enough, and you can use your riding t-shirts instead of bringing more. With a small laundry gel, you can wash more than 50 kg of clothes, and if you ever need more, you can easily buy it from anywhere, they are very cheap. You do not need 2kg of cosmetics; you can easily survive with a simple shower gel, your toothbrush and dry stick. After you go back home, you can return to your normal habits, do not worry you are not going to die from that.

Number 4

Planning too many or too little kilometers per day. In the first scenario, you have to ride many hours and you cannot enjoy the trip. In the second, you will move slowly, and you will need more time. In both cases, the result is not going to be what you expect.

Riding and working at the same time. The idea is very simple, you ride all day and later in the evening from your smartphone, tablet or laptop; you keep the business in good order. I have tried this a couple of times. Every night when we stopped, my riding friends were drinking beer, walking around, enjoying the ride, while I was working. The result was a big mess which was very difficult to fix later. Do not even try, it doesn't work, if you can't leave your business, do not go or find somebody to replace you. When you ride, you have to be concentrated on the ride and not on the business; only then you can really enjoy the journey.

******

Top 10 tips to stay Warm and Dry on a Long Motorcycle Trip!

We all know how great it is to ride on the nice sunny days, but it is a different story when it is cold or when it is raining. I will give you 10 practical tips about how to ride in the rain.

If you go on a long motorcycle trip, it is almost guaranteed that there will be some cold days. Maybe rain, maybe rain and cold day at the same time. You have to face reality and confess that there are some negatives of riding a motorcycle. This reminds me of a funny story from one of my trips. I was riding in Spain, crossing the Pyrenees. It was cold, and it was raining. On that trip over 30 days, there were 13 rainy days. Anyway, it was cold, it was raining, and I was riding. Every time I passed the cars, I could see the passengers' faces, and I could almost read their thoughts. They looked at me like I was an alien from a different planet. They were sitting in their comfortable seats, the heating was on, they were drinking tea or coffee and thinking: what a poor boy, is he crazy to ride in this terrible weather? A little bit later on one of my stops, an old lady came up to me and said:

"You young boy, are you okay? We drove past you, and you looked so terrible. Do you have dry clothes? You will get sick, you can leave your motorcycle here, and we can drive you to the first town."

How was I supposed to explain to that lady that it was my decision to ride a motorcycle and I love everything, even the rain? So, I decided to lie. I told her that my final destination was only in 5 km, I have dry clothes and people to meet me there so she could relax and go. The truth is, that I spent another 6 hours in the rain. It was way too much, everything became wet, even my underwear. Later in the evening, I found a nice hotel, and I spread my clothes everywhere so they could easily dry. This was just one bad story to show you the negative side of riding in the rain, but there are some positive stories, and I am going to tell you one right now.

I was riding in Kazakhstan in the direction towards Russia. It was raining all day, I had my gear on and thanks to the gear, I was kept dry, and I was not cold, so everything was great. When I got close to the border, I saw there was a queue more than 1 kilometer long of cars all waiting there. Of course, being on a motorcycle, I just turned left and passed all the cars, but at the end, there were so many cars that I could no longer move. I stopped and began to wait. If you could have seen what I looked like, I was a terrible picture. Standing next to my bike, it was raining, water was dropping from everywhere, but as I said earlier, I was fine. Suddenly, from within the car next to me, a Russian guy came and said: "You shouldn't wait here, you will get wet and end up being sick" He started horning, and he moved all the cars, so I was able to go through in just 10 minutes. I was dry and warm, but it looked like I was in a terrible condition. In this situation, the rain was a plus for me.

Okay, enough stories, let's get to the tips!

Number 1

Rain gear. It is so obvious. Buy good quality rain gear. There is no such thing as 100% waterproof. It is only a matter of time; it could be 5 minutes, it could be 5 hours, but in the end, it will start leaking. When you buy your rain gear, choose a model made up of 2 parts: jackets and pants, the full body suits look nice and maybe will protect you a little bit better, but it is going to be very difficult to wear it when you are on the road, especially if you have big motorcycle boots.

Number 2

Wear it on time. You have your rain gear, and you have to wear it before the rain starts, not during the rain or when you are already wet. Rain never starts from nowhere; you will feel it, see it, and even smell it long before it starts. Do not convince yourself that the rain will be just 2 drops and that your gear will survive, if it is not, it is going to be too late. When you soak your riding gear, it is going to be useless to put your raining coat over the top.

Number 3

Synthetic materials. All of your riding clothes need to be made from synthetic materials. They do not hold water and dry really quickly. You might have already heard the popular phrase: "Cotton kills."

Number 4

Dress with layers. On the hot days, put a t-shirt under your jacket, and when it becomes colder use a shirt with long sleeves, when it becomes even colder you could even put a switcher on the top or something like that.

Number 5

Nice sized windshield. It might not sound important, but believe me it is. It protects you not only from the wind but also from the rain. It is the same with hand guards.

Number 6

Medical gloves. You can wear them under your motorcycle gloves, and they will keep your hands dry and warm. They cost nothing but will make a big difference to your overall comfort.

Number 7

Boot covers. Do not forget to buy these. It is the same story as the riding gear. There are no 100% waterproof boots. The question is, not are they going to leak, but when are they going to leak. With boot covers, you will have a much greater chance of staying dry.

Number 8

Pin lock. If your helmet comes with a pin lock that's great, if not, then you can buy a universal one and mount it on your visor, you will be so pleased when it starts raining.

Number 9

Wind Stopper. When the weather is nice, there are still enough reasons to have one. It protects your neck from the wind, but when it becomes cold or even worse, when it starts raining, you will need something bigger that will protect both your head and neck. There is nothing worse than feeling the drops from your helmet trickling down your back.

Number 10

Waterproof bags. You can buy them from any motorcycle gear shop or hiking shop. They have different sizes so you can buy a big size for your clothes, a smaller one for your socks and a small one for your electronics.

One bonus piece of advice:

If the weather is not good, rains really bad or it is really cold, then wait.

******

How to Cross International Borders with a Motorcycle?

For many of you guys, crossing an international border and riding your motorcycle in a different country sounds like a mission impossible. You do not know anything about passports, visas, documents, languages, and many more. Well, I'm here to tell you that there really is nothing to worry about. Keep reading, and I will give you 10 very useful tips to help you make it easy.

Number 1

Preparation. I will use my favorite phrase again: That preparation is the key to success. Yes guys, the time you're going to spend before the trip will ultimately help you during the trip. It has never been as easy as it is today to get prepared. We have the internet, we have Google, we have YouTube, Facebook, motorcycle forums and many more. Actually, you can find any information you need if you just go online. Make an effort to deeply research the country you're going to visit, check the border regulations, visas, documents, or any kind of requirements they have. You can simply do it by going to the specific embassy website. Over there, you will find all the information you need.

Number 2

Documents. In some countries, you will need to keep in mind that your passport needs to have at least six months before it expires to be able to receive your visa. Do not forget to take your driver license and the title of your motorcycle. If it is not in your name, then make sure that you have a Power of Attorney. I read in many places about international driver licenses, you do not really need it as long as your driver license is written with Latin letters. You might need it if your driver license is written only with Cyrillic, Arabic or Asian letters and it is nothing more than a simple translation of the one you have. You can make it everywhere. In fact, I have been to so many different countries, only maybe one or two asked me to show my driver license. It doesn't mean that you can cross the border without a proper category of riding motorcycle. It might work in 99% of the borders, but sooner or later you will hit a brick wall.

It is a good idea to make a photocopy of your passport, driver license, your visas, your title, and all the documents you carry. You do not need to make 10 different pages or carry a big folder with documents. You can make just a simple sheet like that, passport, driver license information about your visits and that's all, fold it up and of course keep it separate separately in case you lose your documents, this will save you a lot of time and problems should you lose any of the originals. If you do not want to carry all of these papers, just make simple photos and keep them on your phone.

Number 3

Motorcycle and luggage. Your bike has to look like a normal safe vehicle. Make sure that you have light indicators and there are no oil or petrol leaks. Pack your luggage carefully, which means you need to be able to open it at any time if you are asked to do it. If you have locks, then open them before you go to the counter, not at the last minute, you do not have to hold the line and make everybody nervous. It is the opposite way, make it easy for them, and they will be happy. Do not argue with the Police Officers. Give them what they want, and you will be amazed how quickly you will move. Keep your medical kit in an accessible position somewhere on top of your luggage. In some countries like Russia, for example, they would like to see it. It is not because they want to check what you have in the case on an accident, no they're going to check all of your pills because some of the pills are not allowed in Russia.

Number 4

Behaviour. You have to behave like a normal and respectful person. Some of you guys saw me overtaking, splitting the lanes or going in front of everybody at the borders many times, but I never do it in front of the police officer's eyes. To be noisy or arrogant will not help you at all. They have seen almost anything you can imagine. They have rights to hold you as long as they decide and even not let you go in. Be flexible and responsive regarding the situation. If they say move, you move. If they say stop, you stop. Be friendly with them and be ready to answer many questions like: "How much the bike costs?", "How many days have you traveled?", "Where are you going?" What is your top speed?", "Are you crazy to go to this country?" or something like that. Just be ready to answer them, it costs you nothing. It might be very boring for you, but some of these guys have spent decades on that border. They do the same job day after day, watching the same line, so when somebody like you turns up on the scene with a motorcycle going to a different destination, it is like entertainment for them, and they will want to ask you questions, just answer them. Be polite, talk with them, give them some sticker or souvenir from your country and this will open all doors for you, I promise you that.

Number 5

Corruption. In some countries, this is still a big problem I will say it is like tradition. We have a saying for this in Bulgaria: It doesn't matter how expensive the cigarettes are, we are going to smoke and it doesn't matter how cheap the petrol is, we're going to steal it. Some things cannot be changed. It doesn't matter how desperately we want it, it will be like mission impossible, and it will cost you a lot of waiting hours at the border. I will tell one personal story. It was a long time ago in 1999, in Greece, at the Albanian border. I was waiting to go in, and my friend was a day behind me. We were told how exactly the border works, how much I have to pay, so without even thinking about it, I found the proper men, paid what I had to pay, and he let me go in within just 30 minutes. On the other hand, my friend decided that this is not right and he refused to pay anything. It cost him 24 hours at the border, and in the end, he paid the money and went in. So you tell me, what is that time worth it? But this was just one case, it doesn't mean that every time when you see 20 cars in front of you, you have to offer money, as I said before, be flexible and act regarding the situation. If it is the matter of money, do not worry, they will tell you, you will know.

Number 6

Customs regime. In Europe it is easy. You just fly from country to country, and only the information signs change their language, but when you travel outside of Europe, it is a different story. In most of the borders, we have to fill a form for preliminary import.

It is basically a declaration from you that you're entering that country with the specific motorcycle brand, model number, all the information you have in your title. You will also need another declaration about what you are carrying with you, you just have to sign it, and then you're free to go. Of course, you'll receive a copy, which you have to keep with you until you leave the country with the same bike. And something else that is very important; you cannot leave the country without the bike. Do not even try, you will be arrested. That's why last year in Morocco, when Dima fell down and broke his leg, he needed to ride the bike 1000 kilometers to the Spanish border because he couldn't leave the country without the bike. There are some different countries like Iran, Pakistan, and India where you will need a different type of customs regime. The name is TIR Cartnet. It is a little bit more complicated and you have to receive it in your country, you can read more about it on Google.

Number 7

Money and insurance. In most of the countries, the amount you can carry with you in cash without it being declared is $10,000. If you have more than that, make sure that you tell that to the border police because if they find it later, they have full rights to confiscate it from you. In some countries, they might want to see and check your cash. Do not worry, it is a standard procedure they're not going to steal your money.

Number 8

Insurance. In Europe it is easy. If you have a green card, you can ride everywhere, and you do not even need to worry about it. Every country has different regulations. In Russia, for example, you cannot receive your visa without insurance, but in many other countries, they will ask you to make it at the border. Usually, it will cost between $10-$20, and it will be valid for one month.

Number 9

Weapons. As you can guess, you are not allowed to carry any firearms. You can have a knife, but keep in mind that in some countries like Germany for example, it must not be longer than 12 centimeters, and the blade needs to be foldable. Otherwise, you can be arrested. I read somewhere about a guy who crossed many borders with a signal pistol, but I do not think this is a very useful weapon and I never tried to it carry with me.

Number 10

Alcohol, cigarettes, and drugs. You are allowed to carry only one liter of alcohol and 10 packs of cigarettes per person. If you're a group, and some of the members do not have anything, then you can split it between you and take more. Dima for example, always keeps his homemade alcohol in the petrol can, a five litter petrol can and the border police never ask what he is carrying in it? I do not need to tell you that it is forbidden to carry drugs on the border. Do not even try. It doesn't matter that you're with motorcycles. They have dogs, the dog will come around, and if you have anything, they will catch you.

I will give you one bonus tip. I should have started with this. The most effective way to cross any border faster is to be friendly, smile and respect the border police and never stop believing in people's goodwill.

******

Top 3 Ways to Arrange Accommodation for Long Motorcycle Trips

As you know, accommodation is a very important part of the trip. Even if you have a tent, you will still need to find a hotel from time to time to take a shower, to wash your clothes or to have a nice sleep in a real bed. Of course, it is not necessary, but I highly recommend doing it because otherwise you will exhaust yourself much faster than you can imagine. On a short weekend or one-week trip it is fine, but on the long trips sleeping every day on the ground could be really hard, and it is going to be the last thing you are going to need after a long days ride.

So, how to find hotels? There are a few ways to do it:

Number 1

Book in advance. Book everything before the trip, you can do almost all of it from your home, sitting relaxed at the computer. Take your time and check out all of the offers, make your choices properly, chose the right hotel, pay everything in advance and so on. If you do it this way, you do not need to worry about anything. When the accommodation is secured, you can focus only on the ride. Sounds good on paper, but the reality is a bit different. When you travel with a motorcycle, it is not the same as going on a holiday with your family. Why? I will try to explain. Your travel time depends on many circumstances. For example, you booked a nice hotel for Friday night; breakfast is included, a great position to be in, absolutely fantastic, and now you can relax. Everything is perfectly planned, but what about if the whole day, it is raining so bad that you have to stop, you have some kind of technical problem with your bike, or even worse you have to stop altogether. You have to cancel the reservation if it is possible or arrange it for the next day. Yes, but who can guarantee that on the next day everything is going to be okay or the day after that, or the whole week.

Another good example is when you planned to ride, for example, 500 kilometers per day but then realise that 500 kilometers is too much or too little. You will have to cancel your reservation or make another one, which is means that you will need a new plan because the accommodation you already booked is now useless. It is the same story when you do not feel well or when you are sick for example, and you need to take addition day off or when your bike is broken, and you need to wait for a part. Then what are you going to do with all of these reservations? Some of them will probably be easy to cancel, but not all of them. So you are going to lose a lot of money.

All of this could happen when you travel alone. When you have a riding friend, the chances are doubled, unless you are thinking to leave him there because his problems do not concern you at all. The more you think about it, the more clear it becomes that booking in advance is not a very good option for a long motorcycle trip.

Number 2

Book online when you travel. Yes, you can do it very easily. You can use one of these big websites like booking.com or hotels.com. You can even download their apps, use your location service and make the reservations a day earlier, the same say or even at the last minute. For every one of you who want to secure their hotels, I highly recommend you to use this option instead of booking everything in advance. It is much better, and you are not going to waste all your time, efforts, and money; here comes the important "but." There is no guarantee that you will be able to make it on the day of the bookings, even if you book them at the last minute, because all of the problems I told you about still exist even if you have only 200 kilometers to your desired destination, yes, you still might need to cancel it. Another con of this type of booking is that you do not know what you are going to get. For example, 3 stars in Germany are not like 3 stars in Bulgaria. The quality standards are different. Usually, the pictures and the descriptions on the website do not match with the reality. They use a very good photographer to make the perfect pictures of the rooms to give you the idea that it is a great huge room and then when you go to the place, you find out that your room is the size of a toilet.

A few times I made this mistake of booking a hotel in advance, and when I got there I found out the hotel was not as described, I had to pay an additional price for parking, and the city centre was far away. Later when I walked around, I found so many nice hotels in better positions which were even cheaper than mine, but I already booked and paid. The biggest con of online bookings is that not all hotels are listed there. Even in Europe in small towns or villages, there aren't any listed. What about if you travel outside of Europe, to Asia, Africa or South America? How are you going to find your hotel? How are you going to book online if the hotel is not there? I will tell you how.

Number 3

Find a hotel when you get there. It is very easy. Why do you have to worry so much about something so obvious? The hotels, motels, guest houses or hostels have existed for hundreds of years. How did people find them in the days before the internet? What do you think Ted Simon did in the 1970s or the guys from "Enduro Mondo" did in the 1990s? In the worst scenario, if I do not find a hotel then I have my tent, but this has never happened. In all of my trips, I have only booked a hotel online a few times.

There are so many things to worry about on a long motorcycle trip that the accommodation is not on my list. If everything is safe and secure and planned out exactly in advance, where is the adventure?

******

Motorcycle Crash Bars and Crash Protectors. Are they really worth it?

Are motorcycle crash bars really worth it? The answer is both yes and no. It really depends on the type of motorcycle you have, and the accident you are involved in. I do not have a simple answer for you guys, but I can tell you what I think.

The usual advice will be that if you plan to travel the world, you will definitely need it. In the case of an accident, it will protect your motorcycle from serious damage. This statement could be absolutely right but also could be totally wrong. Let me explain why.

There are a few types of motorcycle crash bars.

sliders. They are usually recommended for sports bikes. They are massive metal cylinders or other shapes usually mounted on the frame or on the engine. The idea behind them are that if you slide down, they will leave the most important parts of your motorcycle untouched or at least protected from serious damage. I have seen that they really work well. The main reason they work so well is that they have a large diameter, they are short, usually they are supported with big bolts, and it is almost impossible to bend them.

The second type which is much bigger are sliders that are made from bent pipes. They are designed to protect your engine, radiator or cylinder heads. The most famous which you have probably seen is on the BMW GS 1200. Of course, there are many different sizes, models, and options for almost any bike.

The third type is more likely to be seen and used on adventure bikes. They are designed to protect the engine and also the side of your motorcycle. You can find tons of picture and video evidence that they work really well. There are thousands of models, and you can find and chose the one which is suited to you, your motorcycle, and your wallet.

There is another type which became more popular in the last few years, mostly after the new GS 1200 adventure was launched. It is the combination of the bottom and top part, and in some models, it is going around the bike, even under your headlights. The idea behind all of this is to protect your motorcycle from any accidents.

So, guys, the question is still there. Do they really work and is it worth spending the money for crash bars? The answer is not that simple. If I say that they work, you are going to ask me why I do not have them on my motorcycle. If I say, they do not work many of you will attack me with evidence that they work and that it is much better to have crash bars. Who is right? Everybody is right. It really depends on the type of motorcycle you have and the accident you are going to be involved in. For example, on a GS1200 the crash bars are a must because if you go down, you will probably break your cylinder heads, but on my bike, they are not necessary. This is not because I am a big pro, but because my bike crashes pretty well, actually nothing really happens only scratches on the tank covers. As you already know, I spend a lot of time and effort to remove weight from my motorcycle, and it will be very stupid to add it back with crash bars because some of these crash bars weigh up to 10kg. On the other hand, if I had a GS 1200, then I would definitely use them because it is very important to protect the engine.

I am sure you can find more than enough video reviews of the crash bars model you want to buy. As you already know, the most important part of any crash bars and of course the weakest point of it, is the mounting system. It is very important for the crash bars to be mounted properly. I have seen so many poor designs. For example, a few years ago I decided to buy one for my motorcycle. On the pictures it looked absolutely great, it was not so big and in the description, it was said that it was light, so I ordered one without even seeing it. I was told it was going to be strong enough to protect the bottom part of the engine and the radiator in case I go down. I am not going to tell you the brand because it is not important, but when these crash bars arrived, I was surprised. The pipe was fine, but the mounting points were so poorly designed that I spent more than 2 hours just trying to mount it on my bike. I had to remove 50% of the parts around the engine to be able to mount it, and from the moment I installed it, I immediately realized that I had made a huge mistake.

It was obvious it was not going to work the way it was described. It was more likely to cause more damage than provide any real protection. It was supported only on 2 spots which meant that if I went down, it would bend immediately because of the weight of the bike. The distance between the actual pipe and my engine cover was 2mm, so instead of scratching my tank panels I could break my oil filter cover, water pump housing or even break the cooling reservoir. I kept it there for a couple of months, not because it provided any kind of protection but because I couldn't remove it. The next time I needed to work on that side of the bike, I removed it. One of the mounting holders is still there because in order to remove it completely, I have to take down the whole engine. What I am trying to say basically is that the crash bars will protect your motorcycle, only if they are designed and mounted properly. Do you think that a 2mm rail will hold the rail of a 250 or 300kg bike? Or, that 6mm bolts will not bend when you go down? The laws of Physics are clear, and you do not have to be a Professor to realize that the heavier the bike is, the better design and stronger holders you will need. Otherwise, they will protect your motorcycle only if you drop it on the side with no speed. It will be much better if your crash bars are on the frame as the engine. I will also suggest that you buy a proper handlebar which is at least 28mm and also handguards with a metal frame in because then, you can be 100% certain that when you hit the ground, the handlebar will absorb most of the impact energy.

******

When the Adventure goes wrong

When the adventure goes wrong. That was an interesting title. So, now you're curious about what exactly is happening. Do not worry, it's nothing special. I am going to tell you some funny and some not-so-funny stories from my trips.

A few breakdown situations, extreme heat, high elevation, food poisoning, lost passport, burned clutch and one broken leg in the middle of the Sahara Desert. I will try to give you some very useful advice about what you have to do when the adventure goes wrong.

We all plan our trips well. Prepare for the worst but expect the best. That's a wonderful phrase but sometimes shit just happens. Whatever you need to face, please do not panic and stay as calm as possible, always give yourself enough time to find a way out. A friend of mine used to say, "There are no problems, only solutions" and he was right. If you step out just for a second and look around the whole situation, you will realize that it is not so bad, it could be much worse.

People always ask me "What are you going to do if your bike breaks down?" What a stupid question. I can ask you the same "What are you going to do if your car breaks down?" You're probably now going to tell me "I do not know, I will try to fix it, and if I can't I will go to the garage ". My answer will be "I will try to fix it if I can't I will try to find a garage" and you probably will say "Yes, but you are on the road". And, where are you? In your living room? It is exactly the same, there is no difference, but you will still resist "Yea but you are in a different country". What is the difference between different countries? The people are people, the garages are garages, and the mechanics are mechanics. There is no difference.

What you have to do is just to try fix your bike if you can't look for help. There will almost always be people who will be happy to help you. Many small problems could be fixed without any help, but if you have something major just ask for help and you will receive it. I can tell you one funny story.

So, we were 2 people riding in the Karakum Desert, Turkmenistan. My friend had no off-road experience and the sand was his worst nightmare. So, from the moment we got to the sand he was in shock. Yes, it was very difficult for me as well but somehow, I managed to go through that san. Because he was in a stressful situation, for him it was very difficult. So, to go through the sand we spent more than an hour just digging around and pushing, lifting, holding the bikes and so on. Finally when we got out of that sand we just stepped on nice stable surface and he said, "Well I think we have a big problem" and I said "What are you talking about ?" and he said "I lost my passport" and I said "What ! Where was your passport?" and he showed me his pocket. I would never use such a pocket to keep my passport. I asked him "Are you sure the passport was in your pocket before we went through the sand?" and he said "Yes, yes I am sure the passport was in there." So, my first impression was "What we going to do now, we are in the middle of nowhere, we have no passport, where can we find the Bulgarian embassy? " and then I told myself "Stop, stop, stop, hold on, you do not need all of this shit just think, calm down and think." and then I realised at it was only about 2 kilometres of sand, there is nobody there, it is only one road, maybe it is somewhere on the sand. So, I went back and again and again. I could not find it. The last time I tried I just left the bike and tried to walk. Suddenly from somewhere 2 local guys came with a very light motorcycle riding around and I just shake my hand to ask them for help. When they got closer I noticed one of the guys was holding the passport and he said, "Are you looking for this passport?" and I said "Yes I am looking for this passport". In just a second the problem was solved, but this was not everything for that day.

So, after all of this pushing the bikes, diggings and sleeping, the clutch and stuff like that my friend burned his clutch. So, when we got out of the sand he said, "Well I think that maybe my clutch is sleeping." I asked him "Maybe or sleeping?" but he said he did not know. But after 2 kilometers, we realized that the clutch is burned and needed to be replaced. We are in the middle of Turkmenistan and have no possibility of finding a shop and buying a clutch. So, what we are going to do? Again, do not panic, stop for a while and think about it. We were able to get to the first city, very slowly with a low speed, went to the first hotel and stopped and started to think. Of course, we have been riding bikes for many years, and we both have some mechanical skills. If you do not have any experience, you can call your friends at home and ask them what you have to do.

The solution was very simple in the end, we just put some washers under the clutch springs, and we solved the problem. Actually, he rode with this clutch for more than 9000 kilometers before it completely broke down in Kazakhstan.

And again, we had another breakdown situation. We were sitting next to the road in a big car park, and we had no clutch. So what did we have to do? To stay there and cry or perhaps call a special service to take our bikes and our journey would end. No! Again, we stopped, and we thought about it. I decided to go to the first city and look for help. I had no idea where I was going, what I had to look for, are their shops for this type of spare parts? Probably not, but I was thinking that I would go there, and I will see what I can do. From the moment I went to that city, at the first traffic light, a big car stopped next to me, and the guy came out and said: "Hi, I am a biker like you, do you need help?" I said "Well, yes, I need a clutch and some spare parts. Are you able to help me?" We spent the whole day together. He did everything he could do to help. We went to all the shops, to all the garages, he called all of his friends and checked even their spare parts, but the brand of the bike was rare, and we had no chance of finding this type of clutch. My friend was still standing there in the car park, and while he was there, even he tried to find help, and finally he found it, but it was 800 kilometers away in Samara, Russia. So we still have this broken bike, and we still have these 800 kilometers of distance. We had to find a solution to bring his bike there. The friend I found in the city tried to help me with the transport, and he found 1 minivan. It was expensive, but we had no other choice. When we went back to the car park where the bike was, we had to wait 2 hours for our transport to come. While we were waiting, a big truck stopped next to us, and the guy started to load and unload some stuff from it. It was full to the top with oranges. I asked them if they could help us transport our bike to the Russian border. The said that this was no problem at all and that they could they can help us, but there was only one problem, they were full to the top. We decided to take the bikes down, the front tire bars and everything and load it in one of the side boxes of that truck. So, my friend jumped into the truck and went to the Russian border. I was riding behind, and so we were able to get the bike to the Russian border. Once we got there, we found a clutch assembled the bike and we were ready to continue our trip.

Here is another one example:

We were riding in Turkmenistan and the temperature was over 40 degrees Celsius. The day was about to finish and we had no water, no food, and no idea where we were going to sleep. We were in a very bad situation. We decided to go to the first village and look for help or maybe a hotel or a hostel. We went there and asked, and the people said that they did not have such things in their village. What were we going to do? It was not possible to sleep in our tents as it was over 40 degrees Celsius. One local guy came and asked us what we were looking for. We told him we were looking for a hotel or hostel and he said again that they do not these amenities in the village, but told us to wait for a second because he was going to ask his friend to help us. After 5 minutes his friend came, and he said: "Okay go with this guy and he will help with everything you need." We asked how much is it going to cost us and he said that it will cost us nothing. We started wondering if we wanted to go with this guy, we didn't know him, we were in the middle of nowhere, and these people were strange, but we were so exhausted and tired that we just did it. We went to this guy's house, and we were amazed, it was like a palace. He gave us everything. A big room, all the food we could eat and everything we could have needed. He gave us a nice air conditioned room, breakfast on the next morning and even food and water for the road. So again, calm down, do not panic and believe in the people's goodwill.

Another story:

We were in Kyrgyzstan riding at about 4000 meters above the sea level. Later in the evening, we found a small place to sleep in a local village. During that night I had this terrible stomach diarrhea, so I spent the whole night in the toilet. Early in the morning, I felt like I had been hit by a car. I started to think about what I was going to do about this terrible stomach problem. At that moment the owner of the place we were sleeping in came and asked what is going on. I told him about the problems I had and he told me to stop worrying because he was a Doctor and would give me a pill. Doctor? What are the chances to find a Doctor in this small village where they do not even have electricity. But, the guy was a doctor? He gave me 1 pill, and after just15 minutes I was ready to ride. So once again, never give up, never panic, just think and wait and the answer will soon present itself.

High elevation. Let's talk about a high elevation ride or high-altitude sickness. Some people start to feel it after 2000 meters while others, like the Sherpers in Everest are fine even at 7000 meters above the sea level. For me, the breaking point was after 4000 meters. We were riding in Tajikistan, we spent the night at 2000 meters and on the next day, after a few hours we went up to 4000 meters. It was fast, and the difference was too big. I started to feel bad and had a terrible headache. Even the normal things like the loading and unloading of the bike were difficult. The only way to cure these problems is to go to a lower altitude. The problem was that we had to ride more than 2000 kilometers at that level which meant that for almost a week and we had no chance to make it any faster. Every day I had to push myself to do it. The only moment I felt okay was when I was riding. All of that could have been avoided I knew then what I now know. What you have to do, is take it in stages. For example, if you plan to ride up to 3000 meters, then you have to come back 500 meters and spend the night or sleep at the 2500 meters point. Then, on the next day if you feel well you can go, if you do not, you have to stay until you feel better. After that, on the next day if you plan to go to 4000 meters, ride to 4000 meters then come back to 3500 meters, and spend the night there. If you feel good, you can keep doing it.

During this time you have to do some exercise so that you are giving enough oxygen to your body. Just walk around, go for a simple run, or hike a little bit. You have to ventilate your lungs. Give your body enough time to get used to the height. If you go higher without having that in mind, you risk getting serious problems with your lungs and brain.

Do not forget that the only way to deal with this is by going to a lower altitude.

My last example is from Morocco. We were riding somewhere around the Sahara Desert, and my friend fell down and broke his leg. We realized that the journey was over. So, fortunately, one guy stopped and helped us to drive my friend to the hospital and then he brought me back to pick up the bike. It was a small local hospital. They had nothing, they just bandaged his leg and called an ambulance which drove him to the nearest biggest city. He then had to get his leg plastered, and we had to leave him for a couple of days to rest. When all of this happened our first impression was that the journey was over, and we had to find a solution for him to fly home and to transport the bike to the border. Yes, but no. Because he entered the country with that bike, he needed to go out of the country with that bike. He had documents for temporal import. So, when you enter the country with your vehicle, you need to leave it with your vehicle. So the plan to fly home just fell apart. We tried to find another solution. We had the idea of renting a minivan and putting the 2 bikes in inside while one of us would drive the minivan and the other to stay next to him. This was a good plan, but it would not work because we were in Morocco, we weren't in a London Airport there were no minivans to rent, only cars; and the cars weren't an option because he couldn't drive a car with a broken leg. Another option was to find a transportation company to send the bike to the border. We found some, but they were asking for about a $1000, which was more than the real cost of his bike, so he refused. He said that he was going to ride his bike. At the beginning, it was not an option because it was obvious that with a broken leg it was going to be difficult and even impossible, but later we agreed that this was the only option. He drove his bike 1000 kilometers to the Spanish border.

Just a few words at the end:

Do not forget that when you are in a stressful situation, your body and your brain work much better. Be creative, do not panic, calm down you will find a solution. Do not stop believing in the people's goodwill.

******

Motorcycle riding and Life Insurance - Is it worth it?

We always have this in mind when we plan our trips. We believe that when we have our policy, we are 100% insured from any kind of possible disaster. We have this piece of paper in our pockets and now we are free to do whatever we want. Well, I am here to tell you that it is not exactly like that. Keep in mind that everything I am going to tell you today is based only on my personal experience with insurance companies and it should not be taken as an example or as a reason to quit your contract with your insurance provider.

What exactly is insurance?

It is a contract between you and your insurance company that means you are going to give them your money and they will take care of you when you need it. Pay attention to those important words "when you need it". But who will decide on if you really need it, and when exactly you will need that help?

Usually it is an unknown person sitting behind a desk in a big corporation that knows nothing about you. They know nothing about your lifestyle, about your family, and about your problems. To be honest, they do not care at all. He is there with only one purpose: to reduce the amount of money or totally refuse the payment you already asked for. I am really sorry about this, but it is nothing personal, it is just business. More claims automatically mean less money. To make it clearer and easier to understand, I will give you one example from my personal experience.

Many years ago, I planned a journey to Alaska. Because the destination is dangerous, I decided to get some life insurance. I did it, it was nothing special, it cost me something like $30-$40 and no more than that. On the way to Alaska I had to change planes four times. So, I had more than enough time to stay on the plane watching television, reading newspapers or whatever. But finally, I decided to read the terms and conditions of the insurance I just made. I did it and WOW what a surprise. Based on what was said within the terms and conditions I had absolutely no possible option to take any money from this insurance. So, the question is, why I did it at all? Well, I really do not know, maybe you can tell me. As you know in every insurance company they have a list of the situations or the cases they do not pay. When I read all of these points, I realized that with my life insurance, and with the purpose of my trip, I had no possible way to ask for any money.

99% of insurance companies do not pay if you are involved in dangerous activities including car or motorcycle racing, even if you are just a passenger. Driving or riding off-road motorcycles or cars it doesn't matter even if you are a passenger, riding on unregulated roads, hiking in the mountains, even on very simple tracks, ice climbing, rafting or any kind of water sports, attacks from wild animals, flying with small planes, boxing, and the drinking of alcohol. There are many more, but these are enough examples for now. They will pay if you are walking on the street and fall down, but not if you have had a drink before that. They will pay if you have a road accident with a motorcycle or vehicle as long as you have not been drinking any alcohol. They will pay if you have an accident during your vacation in your hotel, if a big brick from a construction site hits you on the head for example, but the owner of the construction company will have to cover all your costs anyway. They will pay if you fly and your plane goes down. But this is the same story as it is already covered by your ticket. If you are traveling by train, subway or any other kind of transportation, it is also covered. Based on all that information, I came to the conclusion that to have life insurance on a long motorcycle trip is just a complete waste of money, unless you are paying some additional price to cover all the cases I mentioned.

******

The best way to prepare your body for a long motorcycle trip

am sure that you would like to know the best way to prepare your body for a long motorcycle trip. Is it running, cycling or even visiting the fitness three times per week?

t is obvious that you will need to prepare yourself, especially your body, no doubt, but what is the best way to do it? Let see the options:

N: 1 - Running

Running is a great way to get back in shape, to lose some weight and maybe fix your high cholesterol or blood pressure problems.

The Ancient Greeks said:

If you are sick, run to cure yourself. If you are in good health, run to avoid sickness. When you are nervous, run, to prevent depression, run, to lose weight, run, to get some strength run...actually for every problem you might have or to prevent every future problem they recommend running.

That's ok, but is it going to help you on long trips? I do not think so.

N: 2 Cycling

Some riders will advise you that in order to prepare your body, especially your ass, you have to ride your bicycle as much as possible. The main argument, is that because both have seats, it will help you to prepare your ass for the long riding days. I cannot agree with that statement. Motorcycle and bicycle seat are absolutely different. The position you have on the bicycle and motorcycle are also different. When you ride your bicycle, you move all the time. This is because you are constantly pedaling. Whereas on a motorcycle, you stay still. The points where your ass is touching the seat are totally different. Yes, to improve your overall health, cycling is great, but do not expect it to help you on the long trips.

N: 3 – Fitness

Going to the gym will make you strong and you can withstand riding 12-14 hours per day without any problems. Yes, it definitely will make you strong. But how much of that power you will need when you ride your motorcycle? If you are totally exhausted after a few hours of riding, it is not because you do not have enough muscles, it is because you do not have a proper riding technique. Fitness is not going to help you on the long trips.

In fact, I know some really great riders who have never been in the gym. One of my friends even told me:

" If we need to run, we should have been born as horses!"

Do not get me wrong, all the activities I just said are great for your body. Ride your bicycle, run or fitness, the best of course is all together. This definitely will help you to improve your overall health, which is very important on the long trips, but you should practice these activities all the time, not just before the trip. It will help you a lot, but not in the way you might expect. To be healthy is great, but it doesn't mean that you are ready. It is only means that you do not need to carry an extra bag with pills.

And now what? Nothing really helps, so what should I do?

I will tell you, but before that let me explain something:

Your body is a very clever biological machine. Something similar would be a super powerful computer. In every moment of your life, this clever machine needs to decide what is the best for you. To split the recourses properly and give you the maximum chances to survive. What this means is that if you run a few times per week, or ride your bicycle, your body will decide that you will need more power in your legs and it will create more muscles on the lower part of your body. If you are a weightlifter or gymnast, then you will have more muscles on the upper part of your body.

It is becoming like a biological lesson and, nothing about motorcycles, but please be patient and let me finish. I am sure that you will understand what I mean.

So, depending on the sport you practice, your body will create more muscles around your legs or around your upper body. How much muscle power you will need when you ride your motorcycle and stay hour after hour on the seat? Not much, and what will your body will do with the useless muscles? It will either eat it, use it for energy or take it back, whatever you want to name it. As I said earlier, the body is a very clever machine and will keep only what you really need. That's why the football players have strong legs and the swimmers have big shoulders.

Sport and exercise are both great and everybody should do it as often as possible, but to develop the proper skills for days spent on long-distance motorcycle rides, will need something totally different.

Now pay close attention here, because I am going to share with you some very important information. The top secret, which every long trip rider already knows, and you are about to learn it. Can you guess what you have to do? What secret exercise do you have to do to become a long trip rider?

You have to ride your motorcycle for as long as possible, that's all!

Guys it is so obvious, if you run you will become a runner, if cycling you will become a cyclist, if you spend much time in fitness, you will create nice body. Can you guess what you will become if you ride your motorcycle?

Start with simple short trips, for just a day or two, then make it longer, over 3-4 days or even a week, with more miles between. Take some off-road trips as well. They will definitely help you to learn how to control the bike on the dirt and after that, to ride on the asphalt will be easy. Try some long distances, 300-500km for one day. With every trip you take, you will feel more confident and will develop the skills you need. At the end, it is not going to be a problem for you to ride 500-1,000km per day, because you have done it before. That's it, so simple - now go ride!

******

96

Motorcycle Trips in Hot Areas

We all know how to ride when the weather is cold. Winter gear, dress on layers, thermo underwear, heated grips and we are good to go. That's right, but what about the hot days, 40C or more? I will repeat - over 40C, not 30, 35 or 38 – over 40C. I will tell you about the 5 common mistakes that most of the riders make, and of course I am going to tell you how to avoid them too.

The problem on the long trips are the constant weather changes. It is very common, if you travel from Europe to Africa or Asia for example, in some regions it will be 15C, perfect for riding with your warm linings on, but after few days it might jump to 40 or even 46C. If you have never rode at those temperatures before, you probably will make one of the following mistakes:

Mistake N: 1 – Wrong gear.

To carry two sets of jackets and pants is not the best decision you can make. Riding gear, as you know is heavy and bulky. To have an extra summer jacket and pants sounds good, but actually it is not. It will take 50% of the luggage space and then when you wear it on the super hot days you will be surprised how useless it is. Yes, that's correct – it is useless. When the temperature is over 40C and you ride with a summer mesh jacket you will dehydrate yourself much faster than you can imagine. This hot air flow will dry you like a small fish, especially if you planned to ride many km on that day. To undress the jacket and ride only with a t-shirt is even worse. You will burn like a chicken and in the case of accident, even a simple sliding on the road will guarantee serious injuries or perhaps death. The solution, is normal four seasons breathable gear. Of course, remove the linings. Soak the t-shirt with water, close all ventilation pockets and even the Velcro straps around your wrists. Close the vents on the pants as well and have you full face helmet visor fully closed. This procedure will give you 30 min of comfort and after that, you have to repeat it again. It might sound like a crazy idea for you, but I have done it many times and it really works.

Mistake N: 2 – Not having a hydration system.

To have enough water and to be able to drink it all the time is absolute must. In Asia I was drinking more than 10l of water per day. For more than a week I never went to the toilet. Which means, that I did not have enough water. Actually, I was drinking every 15 or 20 minutes while I rode. Can you imagine what it is going to be like without the Camel Bag? And please, do not tell me that a simple water bottle is the same. No it is not, and you can either learn it now or the hard way later on the trip.

Mistake N: 3 – Wrong boots.

I said this story before, but I am going to do it again. We were riding in Azerbaijan. The temperature was 42C. It was a long day and we spent about 14 hours riding and then more than 12 hours waiting for the ferry to Turkmenistan. The whole day, I had the feeling that my feet were boiling, but later when we stopped, I started to feel real pain. Finally, at around 06:00 in the morning, we were able to load the bikes and went into the cabin. The first thing I did was to remove my boots. My feet looked like soaked in the water for many hours, but the smell was just unbelievable. Dima, who was about to sleep woke up and said – man – what is going on? Take away this bomb please – of course pointing at my boots. The small cabin with one round window became like a gas chamber. Long story short – the manufacturer said that the boots are waterproof, yes, there were. But to do it, they added a piece of nylon between the leather and the lining. So the boots were waterproof, but not breathable. Be careful next time when you buy your boots. They need to be breathable.

Mistake N: 3 – Too much time between the breaks.

If you normally stop once every two hours, now you have to make it every hour or even shorter. The chances to have heat stroke are extremely high. At that temperature, your body overheats very fast, especially if you do not have enough water. When this happens, you start to lose your concentration and it could be fatal. Stopping often will give you the chance to soak your t-shirt more frequently. Do not play Superman, because you are not. I have seen a few guys try it – unsuccessfully – of course.

Mistake N: 4 – Too much throttle.

I have heard the phrase: It is just a bike, not a wife! Actually, sometimes, when your life depends on it, it it is more than a wife, so be gentle. On the extremely hot days, your motorcycle, the same as you, operates in a very difficult mode. Do not twist the throttle any more than you should. Reduce the revs by 20-30% this will help you to keep the engine and the clutch in good working condition. If you have to wait in the traffic, for example, or you ride on sand and get stuck, turn off the engine, especially for air cooled motorcycles. Keep the tires with accurate air pressure. If it is too low or too high, the tubes might overheat and explode.

Mistake N: 5 – Wrong time.

Riding at the hottest time of the day. It is so obvious but many people are still making this mistake. Learn from the locals. They are active early morning and in the late afternoon. Of course, being on a bike and having a lot of km to cover, you cannot be exactly like them, but at least you can stop for a couple of hours around lunchtime. Usually in the summer, you will have daylight from 05:00 in the morning, up to 10:00 in the evening, so you can complete the km you need for that day. This small change will save your energy and will give you the chance to ride trouble free.

Bonus advice – Wrong meals.

It is a classic to see riders eating big fat steaks or burgers. It is not good to do it even when the weather is nice, but on the extremely hot days is just nonsense. There few very good reasons to avoid heavy meals on the hot days:

1. Meat, fish and eggs are more likely to spoil, because of the heat.
2. Your body will need a lot of water to be able to absorb it, and if you already have some level of dehydration the meat will make it even worse.

3. In some regions, like Central Asia they prepare the food with cotton oil, especially the meat, they actually fry everything in cotton oil. Our stomach is not use to it and the chances to have diarrhea will be double.

So definitely try to avoid meat even if you like it. Do not worry, you can survive for a few days without it, but later you will be so glad that you did it.

******

How to stay healthy on a long motorcycle trip

Long-term riding health problems and how to avoid them. What kind of medication do you have take with you? I am not a Doctor, but I will try to explain it with a few words about what I think.

- What do we have to do if we get sick during the trip?
- What medications do we need to have?
- How can you prevent this from happening?
- Is there any magic trick to avoid health problems on the trip altogether?

I do not know why, but people always expect an easy answer, one super powerful substance or secret exercise to help them to solve all the problems they already have. we have to face reality and confess that our heatlh depends on us, only from us and it doesn't matter where we are, whether it be on the trip or at home in front of the television.

I know that here, many of you will dislike the video or even stop watching it, because they do not want to believe in this simple truth. I perfectly understand that position. I have many friends and family members who are exactly the same and they always need to blame someone or everyone for their health problems. I am not going to judge them, or to reply to their negative comments, maybe they have their own reasons to think that way. I will keep talking because I know that many of you guys think exactly like me and we all together could help to those who are listening to open their minds.

First of all, diseases do not come just like that. They are a long-term result of our everyday life. What we do, how often we exercise, how much time we spend in front of the TV instead of going onto the gym or walking outside in the fresh air.

The second major factor is our food. What we eat, or maybe more accurately, what we do not eat. On that topic I can talk for many hours, but I am not going to do it, because it is not the right place for me to do so. I will just repeat the famous phrase – "You will find your health on the bottom of your plate".

Thirdly, and also very importantly is what you do when you are sick. Just stay at home and take the medications or try to help your body to recover as fast as possible? Make sure that you receive enough vitamins and minerals with your meals. Not only when you are sick, I am talking about your overall diet.

With that being said I will give you some very useful tips:

N: 1 – Do not go if you are sick

To travel on a long trip, you need to be in good health. That is understandable, but what should we do if we are not? Nothing, stay at home and do everything what you can to do to stabilize your health and then you can go. There is nothing worse than travelling on a motorcycle when you are sick.

N: 2 – Water

I repeat this over and over again, and I really hope that you will understand it. 60% of the human body is water. To drink enough water all the time is the most important thing for our overall health. There is one very interesting book named: "You are not sick, you are thirsty" most of the people do not drink enough water. Their excuse will be that they are not thirsty, which means that their body needs less water. Yes, correct, their bodies need less water, because they already adapted to the minimum water intake every day. Which is fine for a short period of time, but it is not good for their long-term health.

Keep in mind that when you travel, especially with motorcycle, you have to drink double the amount of water then what you are used to.

N: 3 – Coffee

The coffee is very powerful stimulant. Actually, some people cannot operate without coffee. In some areas like Central Asia they do not drink coffee. This means that you have to carry some with you for every single day, because the coffee addiction is real, and you do not need to have it when you travel. I personally drink coffee when I am at home, but before every long trip I give it up. It usually takes me one week to adjust my body and after that everything comes back to normal.

N: 4 – Move your body

Sitting for many hours in the same position could be really painful, and could actually, be killing you slowly. It really helps to stand from time to time. I do it usually when I am riding at a low speed, just to stretch my legs and let the blood circulate normally. After a long days ride you have to help your body to recover. The easiest way to do it is to make a simple walk after you stop. Instead of sitting in the hotel, go out, explore the place. Take some fresh air and drink enough water.

N: 5 – Enough sleeping time

Nothing is more important than a good, 8 hours sleep. You will survive without Facebook, Twitter or Youtube. You can check it tomorrow morning or when you come back home. Plan at least one day off per week. If you do not have enough time for it, change your route, plan less km or skip something. It is very important to have enough time to recover otherwise you will have the snowball effect and will exhaust yourself very fast.

N: 6 – More vitamins and water

If you get sick, the best thing you can, is to stop for a day or two, until you feel better. Forget about heavy meals, soups or any cooked food. Drink as much water, juices from lemons and oranges as possible and eat fresh fruits and vegetables in abundance. Give your body enough time and the important ingredients it needs to recover.

N: 7 – Medications

The pills you are going to take with you need to be customized exactly for you and your health at that time. If you have to take some necessary medications for Diabetes, Heart or Blood Pressure problems, make sure that you have enough for the whole trip. I do not have any of these problems and that is why I carry only the basic stuff. Some pills for diarrhea, a wide spectrum antibiotic and a few pain relievers.

N: 8 – Look for symptoms

If you feel that something is not right then it is better to stop on time, and not when it becomes too late. I am saying that, because sometimes people make stupid decisions, especially if they travel in a group. They do not want to be different, to look weak or to slow down the group. They hide their problems and say nothing about their condition until it becomes too late. Do not do it! If you do not feel well, it is better to stop. If necessary, let the group go without you. Your health is more important than anything else.

So, guys with just a few words, your health is in your hands in 95% of the cases. The other 5% is just part of the adventure.

******

The Top 5 things you should never do on a long motorcycle trip

So far so good, you have gained some knowledge about what you have do when you travel with a motorcycle. I really hope that this information will help you to make your trips much easier than mine were for me. Now I will tell you what you should never do on a long motorcycle trip.

Some people never learn from other riders' mistakes, but I will be positive as usual, and I really hope that you will listen with open minds. I do not have any goals to correct you, teach you or change you; I just want to help you.

N: 1 – Never ride fast.

I have said this so many times, but I will do it again. I do not know why everybody wants to have these big, fast, and powerful bikes,100, 120, 150 BHP. On a long motorcycle trip, you need a consistent speed, and not a top speed. It is much better to be very strict instead with this instead of becoming only a fast rider. If you ride at 100km/h, stopping once every 2 hours, you will cover more km in a shorter period of time, than if you ride at 140km/h and stop every hour. Yes, of course if you travel at 140, and stop once every two hours, you will be fast, but how many of you are able to do this day after day without risking getting speeding tickets, causing an accident or even making a navigation mistake. You can make it on the German highways, because there are no speed limits, but to be honest this is the last place I want to go when I travel with my motorcycle.

N: 2 – Never ride with a top case.

I am sure that many riders will attack me now, because they love their top cases, but as usual I will try to convince you to leave it at home. To do it, I have to tell you one personal story with my friend Dima.

I am sorry Dima, but I cannot resist. So, one week before our trip to Morocco in 2016, Dima's Suzuki DR broke the gearbox. He didn't have the time to fix it and decided to buy a new bike. He found one, a Suzuki Freewind, it is the bike he rides now, in small town 100km away from Berlin. In the car, we discussed that the price was too low, that we have to make a proper test and check everything before we bought it. The owner opens the garage and when Dima saw the top case it had he said – that's it, I am going to buy it. It was big black top case with a red reflective line and he fell in love immediately.

When the guy started the engine, it was sounding like crap, but that did not stop Dima from buying the bike. Even when I told him that this noise could be anything from loose clutch bolts to a totally broken bike, he just said – I will fix it, the bike is mine. Just to make the long story short, we took the bike and later we found out that one of the bolts was loose, we tightened it and well done, the bike was great, However, the main reason that Dima bought this bike, was the top case. So, even Dima, who really loved these top cases does not take it with him on a trip.

Do you think that this is by accident? No, it is not. The top cases are great to ride in the City, to store all your stuff, even the helmet, but on the long trip they are pain the ass. After many riding days, you will need to change some bolts on it, to fix the broken holder or sub frame. If you plan to take an off-road section, it is almost guaranteed that you will break it or lose it all.

N: 3 - Never take spare tires with you.

They are too big and too heavy. In the best scenario they will weigh about 10kg. If you have a big adventure bike, this could even be more. Because of the shape, you need to put it on the top of your bags, or on both sides of your hard cases or saddle bags. In both cases, you will have difficulty accessing the stuff on it and each time you need something, you have to remove it. Also, as I said earlier, they are too heavy, and you need to tighten them really well. But because of the weight, they will move all the time and you need to stop and re-tighten it again and again. I did it only once for about 2,000km and that was enough for me to learn my lesson. Ok, but what do we have to do when the trip is long and we need it?

Great news, there are few options:

Number one - chose tires to last the whole trip. This is fine, but what about if the trip is a mix between on and off-road? Well, in that case you have to make some compromises or use option number 2, which is to buy new tires when you get to the off-road section. What about if there are no tires? Then you can use option 3 and ship the tires to the destination you going to before the trip. You can send it to friends, or if you cannot do this, some of the main shipping companies offices, like UPS, DHL or another. When you get there, you can change it and continue your trip without having this weight all the time.

N: 4 – Never rely only on your smartphone GPS.

Smart phones are great, and we love them. In this small device, you can upload 3-4 different options, like Google maps, Here, CityGo and so on. They are much easier to use than the standard GPS or paper maps. That's right, they are, but only when they work. The batteries of the smart phones die very quick with location tracking or GPS switched on. The power from the outlets helps, but not always. Sometimes, when you use the GPS, internet, and phone at the same time, the 12V charger cannot really recover the battery. Maybe keep it at some lower-level, but not fully charged. On the sunny days when visibility is not good, it can make the riding more difficult. Another good reason is that smart phones can overheat pretty quickly, usually when you really need it. You can have it as a backup option, but never rely only on it. The simple, cheap GPS will work ten times better than your fancy and expensive smart phone. Do not forget the paper map, they are priceless and always work, even without power.

N: 5 – Never go with loud open exhaust.

It might sound cool when you ride around your neighborhood, but you will definitely regret it on the long trip. When you have to spend many days with all of that sound, you will come to the conclusion which I just gave you, that it is not for you. It will be the same for the riders behind you. Make sure that it has at least a DB killer and Euro stamp on it. In many counties, especially in Europe, the police might stop you, charge you some money, and even not let you continue to ride your bike with this loud type of exhaust.

******

Top 5 Myths about Long Motorcycle Trips

There are a lot of misunderstandings and myths around motorcycle traveling. Actually, if you ask 100 people, then you will probably receive 100 different opinions. Let me tell you the top 5 myths about long motorcycle trips.

Myth N: 1 – It is easy, and everybody could do it!

Well, I am here to disappoint you, and tell you that it is not exactly like that. Let me explain this in a little more detail.

From a technical point of view – yes, everyone with at least one years' motorcycle riding experience could do it. It is not a big deal. There is quite literally tons of information about how to do it, including on my YouTube channel, So, he or she could learn exactly what is needed to make it with ease.

It is also not a problem to gain some mechanical skills and save enough money. There is a video about what you really need in order to go on a long-distance motorcycle trip that you can watch here. As I said, you can learn how to do it, it's easy. The difficult part, or the part that most people have a hard time getting over is the free time. If you do not have it, you cannot do it. In the modern day, we have to work very hard to secure our families and survive in the financial jungle. To have a month or two for vacation will sound like Mission Impossible for most of you. Another aspect to think about, is your expectations from the trip. Some of you will be excited and happy, but some will be disappointed and will never do it again. It is really depends upon what you expect, and your individual point of view.

- What exactly you expect from the trip?
- Do you want to go because you want to see the world, or do you have some different ideas?

This reminds me about something else I wanted to share with you:

Myth N: 2 – You can earn a lot of money from it.

You can write a book or make a film about your trip and sell it later. You can earn millions from it on Amazon, Video on demand or similar platforms. Yes, you definitely can, but if you are Ewan McGregor or Charley Boorman. For the rest of us, unless you are a professional writer, famous movie producer or some kind of celebrity; it will be almost impossible to sell your product. By the way, I have an e-book for sale, you can check the link in the description below, if you buy it now, you can help me to complete my first million dollars in profit.

Another option is to make a YouTube channel, upload your travel videos and get paid for it. Sure, be my guest – for 1,000 views you will get 1$. To earn $100 you need to make at least 100,000 views. I think that you are smart enough to find many different and much easier ways to earn money. What about sponsorships? You can find a blog, company or person to pay for your trips in favor of you making some kind of advertisement. Yes, of course there are many big companies looking for this, but who are you? Has anybody ever heard about you and your trips? How many followers or subscribers do you have on Instagram, Facebook, Twitter or YouTube? How fast and to how many people you can reach with your activities? When you honestly answer that questions, you will understand how far away from the truth that statement actually is.

Myth N: 3 – Long motorcycle trips are very dangerous.

I cannot agree with this, how dangerous your trip will be, depends only on you. You are the man in charge, you twist the throttle and you press the brakes. If this statement comes from the presumption that riding a motorcycle is a dangerous hobby, ok. But, it is also dangerous to ride a bicycle in the city, to climb a mountain, to swim in the ocean, to fly on an airplane, to walk around your neighborhood in the middle of the night and many more things. Yes, but on the long trips, you will do this day after day…and what is the difference? If you are a responsible person, respect the normal traffic rules and human rules, then the risk will be the same as the rest of the activities.

Myth N: 4 - To travel with a motorcycle is very expensive.

For any kind of traveling, it doesn't matter whether that is by bus, train, plane or motorcycle; you will have some expenses. How much exactly depends only on you. You can do it like Arabian Sheikh or like a simple backpacker. You can sleep in 5-star hotels or in your tent. You can eat only in the fancy restaurants or from the local supermarkets. You are the person who has complete control over these things. There is a detailed video about it you can watch here.

Myth N: 5 – On the long trips, it is very easy to get sick or even die.

When you travel around the world, especially in some countries from the third world, there are some risks of sickness. By the way, not too long time ago, even my country Bulgaria was part of that group. The fair majority of people thought that we did not even have hospitals. I received many questions like: Do you have televisions or washing machines there? I am not joking, these are real questions I received in 2007-2008, not 30 years ago. Many of you make life insurances, every year, because of that reason. A video about motorcycle trips and life insurances is available for you to watch right here. So, people think that if they get sick, then this will be a total disaster/. However, the truth is that in most of these, so-called third world countries, you will receive much better treatment for a very low price or even free.

******

So, Guys, you have now made it to the end of this book. I hope that by now, you feel complete with all of the information you would ever need to know before taking a long-distance trip on your motorcycle, and more! I hope you have enjoyed my stories and more importantly, that you have found the information relevant and useful. Now, I will leave to you to get started in planning your next long-distance motorcycle trip!

If you like the book, and of course if you wish, please write a review and send it to my e-mail: zhelev.p@abv.bg, or write it directly in the Amazon system.

I really would like to hear from you. Just to let you know that I offer a 100% money back guarantee! If you are not 100% satisfied with your order, I will do everything I can to make it right. But if I can't - I will return your money. Take a look on my other book " Head East - Motorcycle Adventure in Central Asia" It is more than 300 pages and more than 200 very interesting pictures. I am sure that you going to like it. Do not forget to visit my Youtube channel and subscribe for a new video every week!

I wish you all the best and always ride safe!

Pavlin Zhelev